Degree of Teachers' Stress
in Jamaica and the United Kingdom:

A Comparative Perspective

Dr. Georgette Bertram

Order this book online at www.trafford.com
or email orders@trafford.com

Most Trafford titles are also available at major online book retailers.

Printed in the United States of America.

ISBN: 978-1-4669-4243-1 (sc)
ISBN: 978-1-4669-4245-5 (hc)
ISBN: 978-1-4669-4244-8 (e)

Library of Congress Control Number: 2012910504

Trafford rev. 01/17/2013

 www.trafford.com

North America & international
toll-free: 1 888 232 4444 (USA & Canada)
phone: 250 383 6864 ♦ fax: 812 355 4082

Contents

List of Figures

List of Tables

Acknowledgments

I would like to say thanks to all my families and friends for their continuous support and encouragement, without which the completion of this book would have been impossible.

Dedication

To the memory of my beloved mother Mrs. Hyacinth Bertram, my beloved father Mr. Stanley Bertram, and my grandfather Mr. Ruel Riley. They insisted that "Education is the key to Success".

Abstract

This study explores the following hypotheses:

1 Stress is common to every teacher in one school or another
2 Teachers in the UK now perceive greater stress than teachers in Jamaica
3 Teachers experience stress for different reasons
4 The occurrence of stress has a negative effect on teaching

Definitions of stress are explored for their values as a heuristic tool and the physiological elements of stress are detailed.

Four theoretical models are offered to facilitate the understanding of how causes and effects of stress may be interpreted by different disciplines, and the implications of choice of models for prevention have been analyzed.

A comparative study was undertaken of the degree of stress in Jamaica and the UK. This was attempted through the descriptive methodology of questionnaires.

The findings were that most respondents claimed to experience and react to a certain degree of stress.

Introduction

Psychological job stress is a growing problem, as the amount of research devoted to the topic in the last decade alone indicates (Kyriacou, 1987). In particular, stress in the teaching profession is becoming a major cause for concern and "teacher stress" was the principle theme of the 1988 annual conference of the NAS/UMT. The union executive had been called on to prepare a detailed report on the ever-increasing levels of stress associated with the job of being a teacher. There was also a call on LEAs to establish standing committees to investigate and advise all aspects of teacher stress. In 1976, the general secretary of the NAW/UWT said that members of the union reported that stress in teaching had worsened in recent years. Teachers felt that the moral support which used to be given by the community had disappeared, and this contributed significantly to stress. In addition, teachers felt that compared with earlier decades, the dominant traditional values of schools were now at considerable variance with those of the wider society.

Staff health, safety, and well-being are relevant to all agencies, organizations, and business concerned with cost effectiveness, output, and service delivery. If an industrial analogy is followed, teachers are interpreted as the productive capacity, the machinery of a school which, without adequate maintenance may slow down or wear out (Pritchard, 1985: 3). Thus the cost of neglecting the workforce in the "caring professions" has a direct effect on the mandated and statutory services and ultimately all service provisions. This becomes a vicious circle affecting teachers and pupils alike.

This book intends to explore the degree of teachers' stress experienced in the UK and Jamaica on a comparative basis. It will give special result from working with the most deprived, disturbed, vulnerable, and devalued pupils in this milieu (Polansky, 1981: 241).

According to a report published some years ago by the Health Education Authority (reviewed in the TES, June 3, 1988), teachers are likely to come under increasing strain as a direct result of government policies. The report identifies the "major shifts of different political persuasions" as being in large measure responsible for the increasing stress teachers are under. In particular, the report cites the policy of allowing schools the choice of opting out of local authority control, the introduction of city-technology colleges, the new public examination systems, legislation affecting conditions of service, school closures, and pupil disruption. The report also points out that teachers are in a high-profile profession where they are often subjected to public scrutiny as mentioned earlier. They are criticized for failing to do something in one circumstance but attacked for doing the same thing in another. Teachers, especially in Jamaica are usually attacked by parents as they feel their children are neglected and need more individual attention. The teacher, as a result of this, tries to comply and is again attacked for paying more attention to some pupils than others. Parents do not consider that the large classes teachers have to work with makes it impossible for them to operate in this manner. There is often no accepted "right" way of doing things. Furthermore, according to this article, there is evidence that teacher-training courses do not prepare teachers adequately for the many roles—social worker, psychologist, psychiatrist—demanded of them today.

Sources of pressure at work evoke different reactions from different people. Some people are better able to cope with these stressors than others; they adapt their behavior in a way that reduces the stress. On the other hand, some people are seemingly more predisposed to suffer stress; that is, they are unable to cope or adapt to the stress-provoking situations. In any case, what seems to be important is the individual's appraisal of the potentially stressful situation, on the one hand, and the physical and psychological response to it, on the other.

It is now possible to observe and measure the effects that mental processes such as perception and feelings have on the body's organ system. We know, for instance, that hormonal changes induce changes in mood, that blood pressure rises to meet challenges, and that the alertness of the brain varies with the flow of impressions transmitted by the environment. Two common complaints made about work are those of overdemand and under-demand, as perceived by the individual. The effect of either type of "pressure" on the body is measurable in terms of the secretions from two of the neuroendocrine systems: the sympathetic-adrenal medullary system and the pituitary-adrenal cortical system (Frankenhaeuser, 1979). This is not the place to go into neurophysiological matters. The general point to be borne in mind is that human beings need to maintain adequate degrees of arousal in order to function optimally. However, what is "adequate" for one person may not be for another. Too little stimulation tends to cause distraction and boredom. Extreme under-stimulation may result in loss of initiative and loss of capacity for involvement. On the other hand, overstimulation is likely to result in brainstorming, reflected in an increasing inability to respond selectively to incoming stimuli. In extreme cases, fragmentation of thoughts leading to the impairment of judgment may occur. One other factor which is important to mention in relation to physiological effects is that of the individual's sense of control over his or her working environment. There is empirical evidence to suggest that increased control reduces physiological stress responses, such as adrenalin and cortisol secretions (Frankenhaeuser, 1979). Presumably this has implications for the job stress/health relationship which is, in any case, a highly complex one. Not enough is understood about the biological mechanisms linking stress directly with disease. Clearly the interaction is a multifactorial one, involving personality, genetical predisposition, environmental conditions, and learned behavior.

The writer's interest grew initially out of pretraining experiences in Jamaica, concerning friends and respected colleagues and then her own experiences in the profession. Our work commitment and self-esteem appears to be eroded. The significance of this experience of formerly enthusiastic and highly principled teachers shedding their values in order to survive and continue to do adequate work, with the minimum of damage to themselves, prompted a period of assessment. The ramification of this phenomenon and stress necessitated an evaluation of past episodes, personal vulnerabilities, strengths, and requirements. The result verified the need for support for teachers in the profession. It seems "crucial" to "care" for the "carers" and to "protect" the assets. This conclusion was merely a beginning and subsequently prompted the formation of the hypothesis that a degree of stress is inevitable in the teaching profession, due to the frustrations, conflicts and threats both to person and self-esteem that are inherent in the work. However, much of the stress is manageable, and neglecting to manage stress, or selecting out those who appear to be most vulnerable to it, may have irreversible consequences for both providers and consumers of the teaching profession by depriving the profession of the most dedicated and creative workers.

In this book I have explored the degree of teachers' stress in Jamaica and the UK on a comparative basis from within the combined framework of my own questionnaires and articles done by researchers.

The hypotheses proposed are as follows:

1 Stress is common to every teacher in one school or another.
2 Teachers in the UK now perceive greater stress than teachers in Jamaica.
3 Teachers experience stress for different reasons.
4 The occurrence of stress has a negative effect on teaching.

These hypotheses are based on the argument that teachers' stress is mainly mediated by factors within the teaching profession. In order to test these hypotheses, a number of questions need to be addressed. What is stress and how is it manifested? Is stress specific or contagious to particular life stages or age? Does stress affect specific individuals? Are there organizational variables which serve to induce or reduce stress?

Throughout this book, the biologically derived systems theory acts as a framework to facilitate the interpretation of teachers in their work environment.

Chapter 1 examines the entity "stress," seeking to define its effect and exploring its history in order to establish what stress is and how it is manifested.

Chapter 2 is an overview of some of the theoretical perspectives that offer plausible views, explaining sources and effects of stress. This chapter explores how specific or global the experience of stress is and locates occupational variables which might influence the evidence of stress. It also explores at what level it can be solved.

Chapter 3 outlines the methodology of an investigation into teachers' stress in Jamaica, looking at the subjects used and the limitations experienced. Empirical evidence here is confined to questionnaires done in Jamaica but which are compared to articles by writers in the UK.

Chapter 4 then gives the result and analysis of what the research has found.

In Chapter 5 general comments are made on stress and conclusions are drawn.

Chapter 1

Definitions of the term "stress" depend very much on the approach of those using it. Similar terms such as "occupational stress" (Cooper and Marshall, 1976; Kyriacou and Sutcliffe, 1978b; Kyriacou, 1980), "industrial stress" (Coplan, Cobb G, French, 1975) have been used in research related to stress at work. It appears that there is little consensus as to how the term should be defined or as to the model of occupational stress that should be employed.

Kyriacou and Sutcliffe (1978b) distinguished two major approaches to understand the nature of stress at work. The first is an engineering model. It defines stress in terms of the stimulus characteristic of the environment and stress is seen as a pressure exerted by the environment. Dunham (1984) has put it parallel to Hook's Law of Electricity, the main element of which that are of "stress"—the load of demand which is placed on metals and that of strain—the deformation that results. The second defines stress as a state of the individual and this has been labeled as the physiological model (Cox, 1975). This derives from the early work of Seyle (1956) carried out with reference to the response pattern of the individual. This model has been even more widely employed (e.g., Appley and Trumbull, 1967; Arnold, 1967; Cofer and Appley, 1964; Dohrenweld, 1961; Levi, 1972; Pepitone, 1967; Scott and Howard, 1970; Sells, 1970).

Most of the authors, with the exception to Arnold (1967) who defines stress as any condition of disturbed normal functioning, qualify their definitions of stress as a state of the individual, with respect to what the state is, a result of, or response to. Levi (1973); Seyle (1974) considers that the state consists of non-specific responses of the body to any demands made upon the organization. Others have argued that stress is the result of an imbalance or discrepancy between demands and ability (Growler and Legge, 1975; Welford, 1973; Morris, 1975). Definitions of this type have been labeled transactional models of stress (Cox, 1975). I intend to explore these and other models as seen by other researchers later on in this chapter to show a better understanding of stress.

Kyriacou (1986) further suggests three important factors which seem to make teachers more prone to stress. The first one is the feeling that they are required to meet a high level of demands (either from significant others such as the headmaster or because of self-imposed standards). The second factor is the feeling that they are unable to meet these demands (rather because they lack the appropriate skills and ability or because to do so is not within their control, for other reasons). The third one is a feeling of (perhaps arising from fear of losing face in their own eyes or those of colleagues, or of reduced promotion prospects, even actual dismissal).

This analysis does offer explanation of why some teachers appear to experience more stress than others, in what at face value seems to be very similar circumstances, by focusing on the underlying differences which exist in teachers' perception.

Besides these two models mentioned earlier, there is a third model which I had also briefly mentioned: a transactional model, which focuses on the interaction between the individual and his environment to determine whether stress will occur. This model is employed by some investigator (Dunham, 1984). This model defines stress as the result imbalance or discrepancy between demands and ability as said before. Stress from this perspective means a significant excess of pressure over coping resources. This transaction approach emphasizes the importance of identifying the demands that teachers' perceive and experience as stressful. Followers of this model, according to Dunham (1984), express the view that the extent to which a teacher experiences stress in any situation in school depends upon a number of factors, which include appraisal of demands and his or her own strategies to deal with them; the extent of preparation and rehearsal of the skills necessary for the teachers to handle work pressure effectively.

Though there are many ways to define stress and several approaches to study stress, some focus on characteristics of the environment, others on individual differences in perception and appraisal of situation, and still others concentrate on the interaction between environment and the individuals; they contribute every bit of knowledge to the understanding of stress at work. Kyriacou and Sutcliffe (1978b) tried to make use of the concepts and models to develop a definition and model of teacher stress by which they hope to enable meaningful research into teacher stress. Their definition of stress is "a response of negative effect (such as anger or depression) by a teacher usually accompanied by potentially, psychological and biochemical changes . . . resulting from aspects of the teachers job and mediated by the perception that the demand made upon the teacher constitute a threat to his self-esteem or well being and by coping mechanisms activated to reduce the perceived threat." This definition is conceptualized with respect to the model of teachers stress shown in figure 1.

There are two key points to this definition. The first is "the perception that demands made upon the teacher constitute a threat to his self-esteem or well being." In other words, whether a potential stress (box 1, figure 1) such as disruptive behavior becomes "actual stress" (box 2). If, for example, he is confident that he can cope with the problem himself, or he can call a colleague for help without any reduction in self-esteem, he is unlikely to experience stress. On the other hand, he will feel stressed if he feels he cannot cope with the demands made upon him, or he thinks he could cope with them or feels they conflict with his other values, e.g., he might sacrifice the academic achievement in order to cope with a disruptive pupil.

The other key part of definition is the importance attached to "coping mechanisms (Box 4) activated to reduce the perceived threat." The point is that stress (Box 5) results when coping mechanisms fail to deal adequately with the problem. It implicitly adopted Lazarus' opinion (1966) that stress is the reflection of consequences of coping processes which attempt to reduce threat. Returning to disruptive pupils (which will also be looked at more closely in chapter 2) their models implies that stress results from the teacher's failure to deal with the problem and from consequent reduction in his self-esteem.

Figure 1: A Model of Teacher Stress (Kyriacou and Sutcliffe, 1978b).

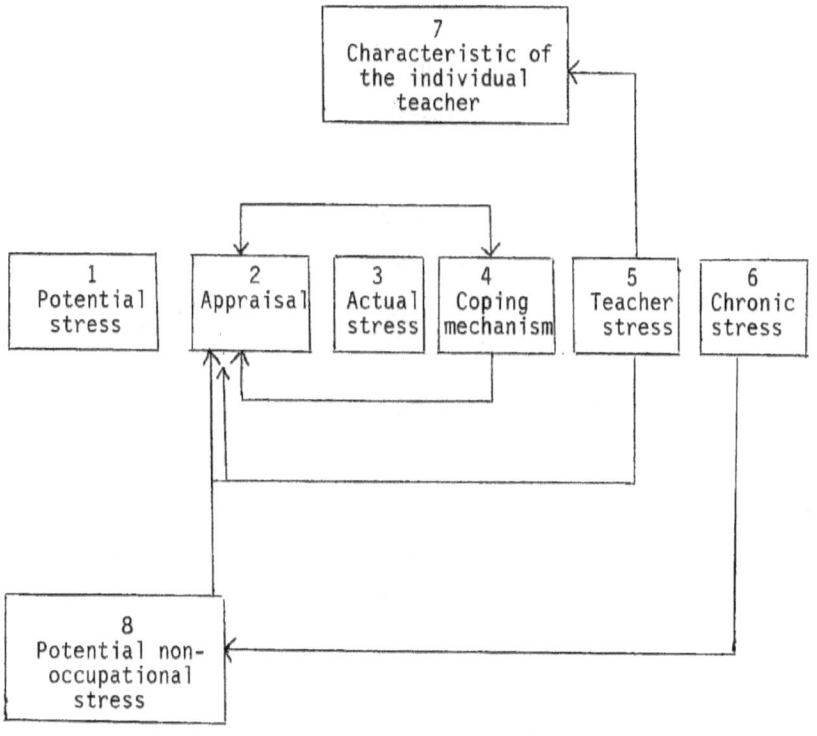

1.1   The Body's Response to Stress

So far we have seen the definition of stress and indicators of stress-inducing factors, but what of the psycho-physiological components of stress? Experiments indicate that stress can be measured through the by-products it creates in the body (Braidwood and Law, 1988). This reaction is common to all interpretations of stress, regardless of the theoretical stance taken. From clinical and laboratory research, largely undertaken on rats, a sequence of changes were isolated in relation to stress and was first described in 1936 as the "syndrome produced by various noxious agencies" (La Haye, 1983: 89). It subsequently became known as the general adaptation syndrome (GAS) or the biological stress syndrome (BSS). This is a primary response often called the "flight of fright" response. One of the first researchers in this field, Dr. Hans Selye, an Austrian-born endocrinologist, located three stages of the BSS.

1   Stage one consists of the alarm reaction, which signals the need to respond to some threatening episode. This is usually a short duration.
2   Stage two is called the resistance stage, which signals the relaxation of the initial acute stage.
3   Stage three is known as the exhaustion stage, a longer stage where the activated system relaxes and absorptions and expulsion systems function (Seyle, 1974: 25).

In humans, a cognitive appraisal of a situation results in the assessment of an impending threat. The brain signals the activation of protective physiological reactions. The endocrine glands are activated. Pituitary and adrenal glands secrete the adrenocorticotropic hormone (ACTH), adrenalin, cortisone, and other related hormones. Neurotransmitters are secreted in the nerve in the brain. Normal indigestive activities are suspended and excretory activities are slowed as the metabolism speeds up. Blood pressure and breathing rate increase along with the release of sugar and fats into the systems and muscle tension increases in preparation for strenuous energy release (Braidwood and Law, 1988; Cranwell-Ward, 1983). This is a generalized response to a wide variety of stressors and can be triggered by anything interpreted as threatening. Physiologically our bodies prepare for urgent action, which in most social and occupational situations is unnecessary. Although threat of violence is a dimension of some work settings, most likely the perceived threat is not real but holds only symbolic significance (La Haye, op. cit., 1987; Simpson, 1987: 3). La Haye suggests that in the form of a challenge or confrontation, the threat is not to our lives but to our ego and our self-esteem. The third stage of the biological stress syndrome, La Haye suggests, is the most damaging. Energy, alertness, and exhilaration may result from a positive assessment of the demands being made, but if a negative assessment is made of the body reaction activated, the length of time that a heightened response can be maintained is limited. The increased hormone production will initially be processed by the absorption and expulsion systems, but may become overloaded. In spite of a seemingly infinite capacity to adapt, continuous pressure along with increased age, renders a body's reactive system depleted. At any time the weakest and most vulnerable parts may break down and may cause any number of the common ailments treated by general practitioners, for example, mouth and stomach ulcers, dyspepsia, constipation, coronary thrombosis, rheumatic fever, problematic menstruation and impotence, headaches, psychoneurosis, hyperthyroidism, diabetes, asthma, the ubiquitous backache, psoriasis, and infections, to name some (Lay Haye, 1988: 99).

Locating the physiological response to stressful situations facilitates our understanding of how stress takes its toll on the teachers. Primary responses are manifest in physical symptoms which are familiar to us all and may include vague feelings of tension, headaches, early waking, or suffering from insomnia and lethargy. Eating habits may change, and there is evidence of increase in dependency on socially acceptable stimulants, such as coffee, cigarettes, and alcohol, which may also be sanctioned by work place culture (Finman, 1982: 17). Emotionally people begin to lack energy and commitment. Motivation decreases and concomitant changes take place in the degree of innovation and imagination involved in the work undertaken. Standards of teaching fall and inevitably discontent and dissatisfaction follows. Caring attitudes may be replaced by ones of cynicism and depersonalization of children, colleagues, and families. Teachers experience panic and incipient depression, irritability, and tearfulness. Self-doubt and loss of confidence follows (Pines et al., 1981). To quote a colleague working in a school in Jamaica:

> "I am constantly exhausted and felt powerless. I never
> seemed to have the strength or the urge needed to
> do my job. I feel a real failure."

Conflicts arise as levels of tolerance decrease and aggression increases. This may be exhibited in the work environment or confined to life outside work. When suffering from stress at work, some people develop the unrealistic expectation that their partner or family will be exceptionally sensitive and responsive to their needs (Cherniss, 1980). Conversely, the family expects attention and rewarding contact rather than intensive involvement in work problems. Seemingly trivial incidents militate against mutual caring, which consequently is gradually eroded. These incidents gradually magnify to cause withdrawal of communication and breakdown of a relationship at its most extreme (Pine et al., 1981). Ayala Pines's (1983: 172) research discovered that people who are suffering the effects of stress at work begin to put pressure on their marriages. The lack of social support systems at work means that those experiencing stress begin to demand that their families fulfill the functions that are not being met by colleagues at work. This awareness that means are not being met, frequently results in a sense of disappointment, which becomes associated with home life and erodes family relationships (Pines, 1983). Although a simplification, the importance of the interface between home and work is obvious here. The home environment can serve to ameliorate or exacerbate work pressure and work unrelated leisure activities act as a great and valuable release of tension (Tapp, 1986).

There are numerous difficulties associated with work in a postindustrial society as organizations change, gradually and pragmatically, in response to demand and technology vagaries. Greater automation means that organizations undergo periods of enforced change, and adaptation in work patterns and attitudes follow. Change is rarely unproblematic, often engendering discontent and alienation of the work force, low motivation, and lack of cooperation. Head teachers and unions conflict with each other as do other groups in the work force, especially in Jamaica. Teachers are making one demand for which the union representatives are saying "no"; we have to make demands that the government is likely to accept. Demand for more salary does not depend on the teachers' choice; neither is consideration given to the state of the economy. It has always been the government's decisions which normally result in teachers going on strike or work to rule. A plethora of theories exist to substantiate the machinations associated with conflicts at work, ranging from the political, social, psychological, developmental, and future shock explanations to broad social perspective, Marxist, organizational and management, individual personality, and helping relationship theories (Handy, 1976). Early management theorists, however, understood the answer to many problems of the workforce, such as motivation to be directly related to the financial remuneration offered. It is now recognized that workers do not respond passively to working conditions imposed on them but react constructively and creatively in attempts to derive an intrinsic satisfaction from work to meet their own needs (Argyle, 1974: 91). In studies of assembly-line workers, individual creativity was witnessed in many ways: from practical joking to adjusting output and controlling rates of production, modifying jobs, and setting individual goals. At the opposite end of this spectrum, dissatisfied workers allow the machines snarl up or break down and direct sabotage was identified (Sayles and Strauss, 1966: 20). Argyle suggests that this was permitted by the subculture, which embraces the workplace, permeating it with its own social organizations, ideas, rules, and morals, encouraging certain behaviors, personalities, and motivations (1972: 13). Unemployment research tells us that for most people, possession of a job is a salient part of their lives and that boredom and depression emanate from having no occupation (Hawkins, 1979). This stems from the perception of time, the low level of stimulation, lack of satisfying activities, and the cognition of constraints placed on the individual (Guest et al., 1978).

The complex facets of work experience alluded to here including motivation, satisfaction, rewards, conflicts, control, stimulation and challenge, autonomy, and personal. Psychology indicates a complicated interrelationship and interaction between teachers and their environment. Consequently, the casual relationship with stress is multifaceted, but the literature indicates the organizational variables, including work culture, may permit or deny the existence of stress and may also serve to induce or reduce stress. That is, teachers are not simply a reflection of work or social currents or of the psyche, rather there is a dialectical interaction between them.

1.2   **Models of Stress**

There are a number of models that have been explored by researchers while looking at the definitions of stress. I have chosen four of these models to give an overview of some of the theoretical perspectives offered to facilitate our understanding of the causes and effects of stress in an effort to create conceptual sense out of a diversity of theories. The medical mode, which most researchers have discussed, looks mainly at the body response to stress from a physical and psychological point of view. The Marxist model, which is self explanatory, sees stress from a political point of view, looking very closely at the governing bodies. The transactional model by Cox (1975) maintains that stress will occur as a result of the interaction between the individual and his environment whereby failure to meet or cope with demands made by the environment has important consequences for the individual (Burgoyne, 1975; McGarth, 1970;

Sells, 1970). However, the transactional, though similar to the ecological models, are basically qualified physiological models as they still conceptualize stress as a response state.

The ecological model looks closely at the individual, and how they respond to the environment. Different researchers however have different conceptions. The important point to remember is that these models fit neatly into the Jamaican situation.

1.3   A Medical Model

The technical literature presents a variety of approaches to stress; some emphasizing the principles and the importance unequivocal operational definitions or clinical importance. Others identify personal traits or organizational characteristics, while others focus on underlying mechanisms of human development or consequences for the consumer. Historically the medical model has dominated with the approach to stress as a disease, favoring an assessment of described symptoms followed by diagnosis and treatment. The first assumption of this model, that various types of behavior, feelings, signs, and physical ailments can be classified by diagnosis into symptoms, has a number of disadvantages. First, many physical and psychological disorders have no definite boundaries and defy specific diagnosis, and stress is included here. Second, any information gathered to facilitate this diagnosis may initially be fraught with communication difficulties, misinterpretations, faulty reporting, including minimizing or exaggerating symptoms for a variety of reasons. Third, a diagnosis may be unreliable for subjective, judgmental, or cultural reasons of which the individuals involved may be unaware. This is particularly true of gender bias within the medical model. Brown (1986) and Broverman et al. (in Howard and Bayes, 1981), detail dominant patriarchal values that are prevalent and result in a double standard of mental health, which is damaging to women. Labels of "neurosis," "depression," and "hysteria" are more likely to be applied to women than men and twice as many women as men as prescribed psychotropic drugs (Haddon, 1984). The stereotypical bias is reflected in different diagnoses and treatment for men and women with similar difficulties (Broverman et al., op. cit.).

The second assumption of this model is that symptoms reflect a psychological disease (Shapiro, 1981). As we have seen, the essential pathogenic element in stress appears to be that relevant messages about expectations or abilities are being communicated to the defense system, thus undermining functioning.

Consequently, the automatic nervous system and hormonal arousal with resulting pathological depletion and fatigue, increasing susceptibility to wide range of physical and mental disorders (Caplan, 1974: 2). Treating the symptom may have some relief to the sufferer, but stress is not a disease with an organic origin. Locating the amelioration of stress within an orthodox medical model pays no attention to important social and environmental causes. This brings into question the final assumption of this paradigm: the treatment of "cure." Physical and biochemical treatment offered by medical practitioners are known to alleviate some of the more acute symptoms; however, the disadvantages lie in their unpredictability. First, individual response to treatment differs in a way that is not fully understood. Second, treatment prior to change in condition does not prove that the ailment was physical in origin (as research using a placebo has indicated). Third, prescribing the inevitable anxiolytics and minor tranquillizers for stress-related symptoms may have a delirious effect on future coping and may lead to drug dependency (Braidwood and Law, 1988; Gordon, 1981).

The medical model is narrow and restrictive in its understanding of stress. Diagnosis have their use if applied cautiously, but there is a danger that stereotyped or stigmatizing labels, such as "neurotic," "depressive," "inadequate," or "malingerer" may be as demanding as the treatment. Using this model would locate the cause of stress within individual pathology. The major limitations of this approach are in its inability to address environmental and structural influences, personal awareness, coping skills, and the value of prevention and the need for change.

1.4   A Marxist Model

Few things in life are detachable from the political, economic, or social environment in which they exist (Blurket, 1983: 25). Therefore, a political approach to stress interprets on a macro level as well as a micro level. This is to say that both society as a whole and the political system, organization of the individual work experience, are relevant to stress research. The neo-Marxist approach to stress compares it to the phenomenon of alienation and cites it firmly within the capital versus labor conflict (Argyle, 1974: 27). Stress was originally coined in the 1800s during the Industrial Revolution to describe the exploitation by the employers. Workers contribute to the means of production, receiving a wage. The product created, however, generates greater wealth for the capitalist, in turn contributing to the increased mechanization of labor and devaluation of work, by removing the finished article for the laborer. This process has been exemplified in early studies of the mechanization of automobile production lines where operators of the production lines experienced feelings of worthlessness and devaluation. Their tasks became monotonous and repetitive and resulted in employees often not knowing what components they produced or what it was used for (Argyl, 1974; Goldthorpe, 1968; Pines et al., 1981).

A model of alienation can be viewed in four parts: first, there is a "powerlessness." Central to this the workers' relationship to the organization and their perception of individual control over the work processes, autonomy, conditions of employment, influence over policies, and management decisions. An alienative relationship may be generated by the way the "elites" of the organization exercise their power and what consultative role the workers are able to adopt (Smith, 1970: 18). Concomitant to this might be the experience of the workers' distance from the controlling hierarchy and manner of communication. Second, the concept of meaninglessness in work features the inability of the worker to relate to the purpose of the task undertaken or known and how it fits into a complete process. Increasingly, specialization separates out tasks or components of the work, which may be allocated to those with particular skills or qualifications rendering the remaining tasks unrewarding, low in status or meaningless. The third element of the Marxist view of alienation is isolation, that is, not belonging to a working group or not relating to a team or coworkers. Many studies show that satisfaction at work is influenced by positive interaction with small groups of desirable colleagues exposed to similar stresses. Goldthorpe (1968) found that team work did not occur in most factory work, especially in auto-production lines; consequently, it was not rated as a source of satisfaction. This does not, however, eliminate the absence of team work as a source of alienation. The fourth facet of this model is entitled "self-estrangement." This results from experiencing depersonalization or a detachment from work or being unable to regard work as a major interest or means of self-expression (Blauner, 1964). Work is then seen as instrumental for providing remuneration or status.

Self-estrangement may also result from having unrealistically high and consequently unfulfilled expectations of oneself at work. This may be experienced by highly idealistic reformers, or professionals restricted by bureaucratic functions (Anderson and Carter, 1974; Chemiss, 1980).

This model is useful for predicting and interpreting sources of stress within an organization, although individual personality and psychology are neglected, as are the important working relationship with outside agencies and students which are major components of the teachers' experience and other professional occupations. The issue of isolation indicates the importance of team work, which is relevant to teachers. Preventative measures using this model would be piecemeal without radically restructuring society and the capitalist system. Outside agencies, such as government bodies and the society have a great deal of influence on teachers' performance and satisfaction of the job.

1.5   An Ecological Model

Employing an ecological perspective for understanding the complex relationship between the individual and their environment emphasizes the reciprocal nature of all the interacting elements.

Emphasis is not placed on individual pathology but on the degree of disharmony in the person-environment equilibrium (Carroll and White, in Paine, 1982).

To illustrate this model, it is necessary to begin with the small and perhaps familiar element in the ecosystem, the person. Every facet of the individual is an important and influential part of the "person system." Included in this are the person's genetic and congenital factors, temperament, growth and development, personal attributes, such as perception and power of reasoning, coping skills, interests and needs, also the personality dynamics, including frustration, tolerance, self-esteem, and motivation. Behavior patterns are included here, especially those relating to interpersonal relationships, also a person's educational career, degree of training received, and skills learned, their work history, which includes general life experiences, goals, and personal values. The "person system" exists not in a vacuum of course, but within a micro system which in a model of occupational stress is the smallest unit of the work environment; for instance, the office or assembly line, the packing shed, shop or garage, kitchen or classroom (see figure 2). The second level of work environment that impinges on the person has to be labeled the "mesosystem" which encompasses all the micro-systems that form the department or school etc. That is every microsystem of all the individuals at work in that environment (Carroll and White, 1982: 46). The system encompasses all other elements affecting the worker, the family, the local community, any regulatory accountability systems (e.g., funding or managing bodies) are termed the "exosystem" (op. cit.). All other elements of a person's life beyond the exosystem are included in the macrosystem, for instance, soaring inflation of taxes, interest rates, or escalating unemployment, racial or sexual prejudice, ageism, disaster, famine, and other global issues that impinge upon a person to a greater lesser degree. This biological analogy exemplifies the complex forces interacting and impacting on person and environment and illustrates the individuality of the work experience and consequently the stress experience. It offers no answers but does, however, suggest that no single discipline can fully interpret the phenomenon of stress and that an electric approach is necessary to integrate relevant theoretical constructs and to provide a preventative or ameliorative program.

Figure 2: An Ecological Model for the Analysis of Occupational Stress.

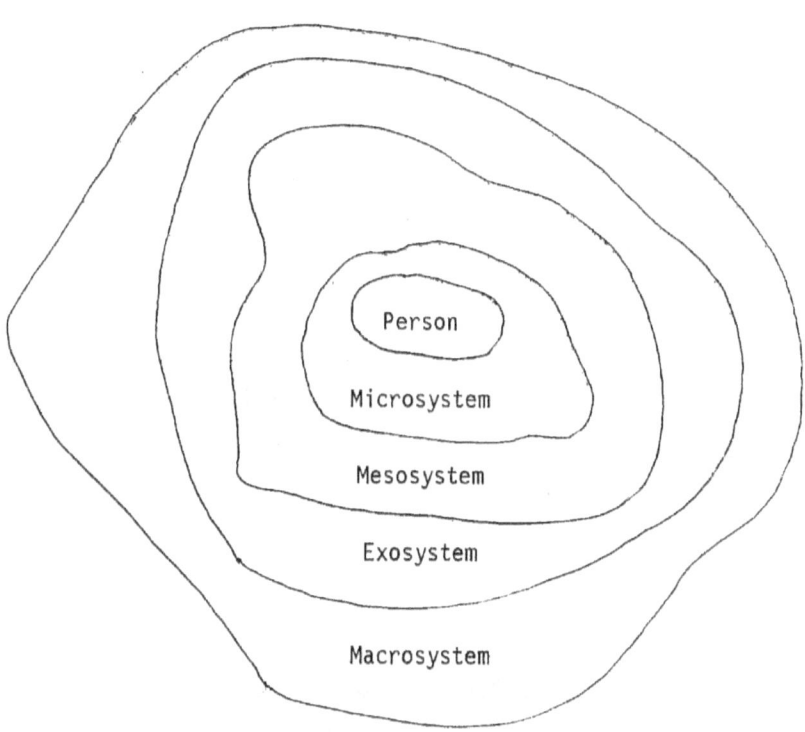

Person	The individual with many facets
Microsystem	The smallest social unit at the workplace
Mesosystem	The larger complex of smaller work unit
Exosystem	Non-worker ecosystem directly impinging on the workers
Macrosystem	The larger cultural and world complex

These elements are complex and dynamic and unique. Interaction continues between all elements and has influence on every aspect of the system.

Carroll JFX and White WL "Theory Building, Integrating Individual and Environmental Factors within an Ecological Framework," in Paine, W. S. (ed.), *Job Stress and Burnout*. Sage, 1982: 47

1.6 A Transactional Model

This model signifies an intellectual convergence of definitions of stress as an individual psychological state, residing in the person's perception of the transaction between the demands on them and their ability to cope with them (Cox, 1987; Cherniss, 1980). The approach concentrates on cognition, which operates as mediator (an interpretive function) between the environment and the person (Bandura, 1977: 59). Dependent on cognition is the individual response, the coping and problem-solving techniques (comparable to Caplan's theory of "mastery," Caplan, 1980: 413). Cox's transactional approach to stress is complementary to that of Chemiss, whose three-stage model has been used as a framework (see figure 3). Stage one features a person's cognitive appraisal of four things. First, of demands being made on an individual and possible consequences of the failure to meet those demands. The demands may be personal ones, featuring statutory duties, required tasks, and changes in jobs. Internal demands include personal desires, goals, values, and commitments. Second, an appraisal is made of one's personal characteristics and resource available to meet the demands, including knowledge and skills, attitudes, and behavior. Third, constraints will be considered, for instance, time, place, and structural and organizational limits. Fourth, assessment will be made of any supports available and received from others in coping. Stage two involves an immediate but shorter-term emotional response to the recognition of a possible imbalance between demands being made and the currently available resources. This stage is characterized by well documented feelings of anxiety, tension, and fatigue. The third stage concentrates on the psychological accommodation of the cognitive appraisal; that is, the recognition and diagnosis of a stressful situation, which leads to a problem-solving process. A solution to the problem may be implicit in its definition or one may need to be generated. This depends on the individual's creativity and repertoire of past successes and failures, models of coping and sources of advice and assistance. It has been suggested that women may be disadvantaged at this stage, possibly having fewer positive role models, resources, and a smaller coping repertoire. This may have been true when this model developed, but situations have changed drastically over the years, and women are now seen to be able to cope better in many situations. This is interpreted as a function of the socialization of women but due also to the nature of the career of many women, largely in traditional caring professions, and often being disrupted by child rearing (Cox, 1987; Pearlin and Schooler, 1978).

Coping then consists of actions initiated to remedy a situation; these are largely cognitive in nature, but are expressed and supported through specific behavioral acts. Chermiss draws our attention to defensive coping as a response to stress, which is described as using detachment mechanisms, such as cynicism, withdrawal, rigidity of routine, and absorption in paperwork. We might compare this to Isabel Plenzie's concept of defense against anxiety, which describes the resultant coping activities as an avoidance type that serves to exacerbate stress (Cherniss, 1980: 19; Menzies, 1960: 109). Coping strategies have been researched by many authors, and Pearlin and Schooler (1978) have established three different categories for these

21

strategies. First, that of social coping; the utilization of interpersonal networks, including family, friends, and colleagues. Second, there is psychological coping, which depends on personality characteristics, especially a person's self-esteem, self-denigration, and mastery. Third, specific coping responses have been identified, which include all behaviors engaged to neutralize or vitiates stress.

This transactional model has proved useful for the integration of much of the stress literature facilitating understanding and utilization of more diverse research. It provides insight into mechanisms used for dealing with stressful situations while offering problem-solving approaches, which may be utilized for stress management. It is mainly reactive in its application and offers no predictive or preventative role.

To apply one of these models in a pure form would be naive as any model is utilized mainly for its illustrative value. Here they serve to emphasize the fact that casual explanations are not simply or mutually exclusive.

Theoretical models, in my opinion, have been found to have value when assessing causes of stress in Jamaica and the UK, while research offers much that promotes interpretation and understanding of the similarities between careers, role and work in the teaching profession that is experienced as stressful. An analysis of stressors in quite different occupational areas emphasizes the role of the bureaucratic and hierarchical organization in employee stress. Teachers in particular, both in Jamaica and the UK, are seen to be highly responsible (although I might add not in all respects) and highly trained professionals who expect pay, conditions, and consultation, which are commensurate with their tasks, knowledge, and qualifications. Yet their autonomy and work experience is directed and severely frustrated by the bureaucratic structure within which they work (Bacharach et al., 1986).

Teachers all experience insecurities and feelings of physical and psychological threat from different aspects of their work. The research indicates that teachers take on many roles in the course of their work, which may include roles they are not comfortable with and demanding behaviors they find hard to reconcile. As in Jamaica, teachers are expected to do extracurricular activities, attend meetings from time to time with no extra incentives in their salary, especially when lack of transportation is at its peak in many remote parts of the country. The behaviors and expectations these roles generate often conflict and give rise to stress. Finally, the research illustrates the complex and powerful emotions which are stirred by working in intimate relationship with students and with parents whose difficulties are enduring and emotive in nature.

A number of models of stress were explored as tools to facilitate understanding of the complex interactions of teachers and work environment. A medical approach was seen to be limited, offering a treatment-orientated model, which concentrates on physical symptoms rather than on the physiological reaction as defined by Selye. Symptomatic treatment concentrating on anxiolytics and tranquilizers identifies personal dysfunction without regard to environmental influences.

The Marxist model was found to be useful with its emphasis on the teachers' perception of themselves within the work situation, being influenced by good communication policies, which promote worker involvement, feelings of belongings, and reduce isolation and estrangement.

An ecological model offering a biological analogy illustrated the need for balance, individual and environmental approach to stress, to fully understand the complexity in operation and to guide ameliorative moves. Finally, a transactional model was included simplifying the structure of personal cognitive appraisals, stress experience, and coping activities which follow. This is a useful model for assessing and planning coping strategies and equally useful for assessing and planning organizational structures to facilitate coping as can be seen on figure 3.

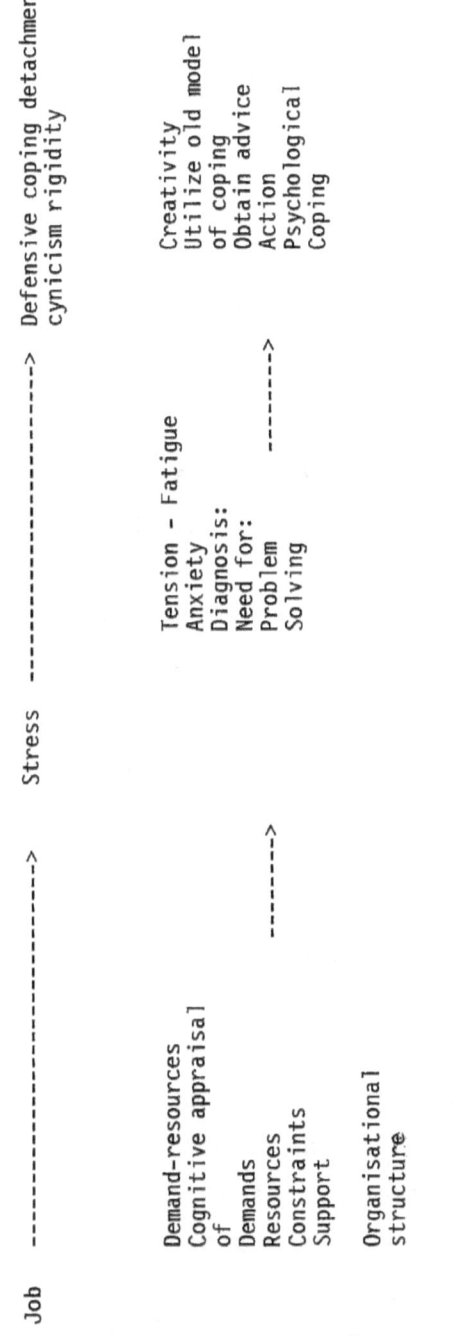

Figure 3: Transactional Definition of Stress.

Job ------------------> Stress ------------------> Defensive coping detachment cynicism rigidity

Demand-resources
Cognitive appraisal
of
Demands
Resources ---------->
Constraints
Support

Organisational
structure

Tension - Fatigue
Anxiety
Diagnosis:
Need for:
Problem ---------->
Solving

Creativity
Utilize old model
of coping
Obtain advice
Action
Psychological
Coping

Cox T "Stress, Coping and Problem Solving" (1975), Work Stress (1987: 6)

Chapter 2

Review of Literature

2.1   Introduction

The array of models available to promote prediction, understanding, and prevention of stress is an indication of the many problems associated with researching stress. Mackay and Cox (1979) cite the lack of government action or encouragement as a major problem for researchers. There has also been the tendency to adopt a differential focus, for example, on either work or stress, with little attention to the interdependence of these factors. There are particular problems inherent in identifying the incidence rate of stress with definitions being one of the problems. Chapter 1 relates to the physiological effects on stress; however, there is a great deal of ignorance in the layperson of the many illnesses and complaints that may be stress related (Cranwell-Ward, 1983). Interpretation of depression, insomnia, feeling rundown, premenstrual tension, ulcers, and other symptoms therefore have Implications on teaching and may be stress related. Further obstacles to identification exist, which are exacerbated in professional occupations by an ideology that inhibits disclosure. This ideology assumes certain rights and privileges along with a degree of expertise, which generates the ethos of emotional maturity and occupational competence (Bacharach, Beuer and Conley, 1986). Attempting to maintain the idea that self-esteem is dependent on confidence overrides one's concern for health and well-being and resist disclosure (Fisher in Farber, 1983). Following a psychoanalytic approach, Fisher (op. cit.: 44) suggests that this demand arises from the fear of being revealed as a "sham" or incompetent.

In an article that analyzed stress among teachers in forty-two elementary and forty-five secondary schools in the US, the authors concentrated their evaluations to a greater degree on an organizational analysis of stress. They emphasized that stress resistance is a personality trait, but that stress stimuli are characteristic of the organization (Bacharach, Bauer and Conley, 1986). Their research findings appear to collaborate the argument of distinct differences in stressors for secondary and elementary school teachers, which indicated organizational differences. However, role conflict correlates highly with stress for teachers. Dunham (1976) from his investigation on teachers' stress among 658 teachers in primary and secondary schools in the UK found that the reorganization of secondary education was accompanied by an increase in teachers' stress and also that severe stress was being experienced by more teachers.

This can be compared in Jamaica with the students' feelings sudden teacher changes, but for teachers this stress was expressed in terms of political deviousness of the government and anger at the inadequacy of communication over changes (Fineman, 1985). With regard to this, teachers' inadequacy of training was also cited as a stressor, leaving teachers unprepared for the realities of work. Feelings of threat and risks attached to the work, as Rutter and Fielding describe in another case of situational stress, also feature in teachers' descriptions of stress. The threat of being at risk is important to the individual's concept of demands made on them. Sources of threats and the risk of "failure" were expressed as being exacerbated by current public attitudes and media representation. Fineman's study suggests that sources of stress for teachers are intrinsic to their occupation. The conflicting roles of what teachers are expected to do and what they actually do and threatening and frustrating elements of the organization are particularly stressful. Teachers, especially in Jamaica are expected to conduct devotions, being the leader of a school house team, although they take objections to doing so. They are accentuated by elements that are extrinsic to the job. This is supported by Smith (1970), who cites the organizational setting, restricted autonomy, tiresome administrative procedures, and limited resources as factors which undermine teachers' provision, and Brookings et al. (1985: 147), who find relationships with supervisors and colleagues' rates of pay and conditions as adding to the frustrations and stressors of work in the profession.

An earlier paper by Fineman and Payne suggest that much of the evidence has related stress to role conflict and has been methodologically created. However, Cooper (1983), Rutter and Fielding (1988), Gutck, Nakamura and Nivea (1981), Fineman (1985), and Bacharach et al. (1986) clearly related stress to role conflict and ambiguity.

Factors identified by stress theory (e.g., Cox and MacKay, 1976) as important in the process of cognitive appraisal of the work situation include freedom in coping and support in coping.

Passive jobs are associated with low demand and low discretion, which tends to lead to loss of ability to make decisions, solve problems, and tackle challenges. On the other hand, active jobs are associated with high demands and high discretion so that the challenge in the job is balanced by the possibilities for alternative methods of dealing with the situation. Problems can arise, however, when there is no satisfactory action that can be taken. MacKay and Cox (1987) make the point that high demand with control indicates effort but not distress. Clearly teaching falls into the category of an "active job" that is one with high demand and, for the most part, high discretion. Despite this, it is not uncommon in any experience to find teachers citing boredom as a source of stress in their professional lines (Wade, 1988). Behind this lie such factors as the high amount of marking required in certain subjects, the large number of meetings to attend out of school hours, and the increasing number of reports (concerning government initiatives, etc.) that have to be read and commented on.

In a review of teacher stress carried out by Kyriacou and Sutcliffe (1977), it was found that in the UK, little attempt had been made to measure the extent to which teachers feel they are experiencing stress or to identify the aspects of the teacher's job which are regarded as stressful.

2.2   Understanding Stress

There has been a steadily growing interest on the effects of stress on teachers in the UK, particularly since the reorganization of secondary organization in 1975 and the implications of this stress for their practice. Dunham (1975), Kyriacou and Sutcliffe (1978a, b), and Cox and Brockley (1977) have all studied teachers' stress from different perspectives and all have concluded that teaching is a stressful occupation. Although many of the researchers cited below have focused on pupil behavior as the main cause of stress, they have also highlighted other issues as net contributors to teacher stress.

Fletcher and Payne (1982) also viewed stress as a consequence of the practice of teaching. They suggested that the outcome (the degree of stress) will depend on three key factors: job demands, support, and constraints.

Fletcher and Payne (1982) argue that a teacher who may be subjected to a high level of job demand may be compensated by high levels of support and low levels of constraint. Unfortunately, they do not state the type of schools or localities; other than that, the subject of their investigations was schools in Midland towns. The above scenario may be a reality in a small junior school with a highly integrated staff, where they are good at communication. However, in a large comprehensive school where these features are not prevalent, the teachers may find that the demands are high, with little support and much constraint. In Fletcher and Payne's sample, 22 percent replied positively to the questions asking them if they ever felt they were going to have a "nervous breakdown." All thirty-four individuals (22 percent) had taken medical advice, which confirmed the seriousness of their problem.

Kyriacou and Sutcliffe (1978a, b), using a questionnaire survey, investigated the prevalence and sources of stress and ill symptoms among 257 teachers from mixed comprehensives in England. Essentially their study was designed to answer a central question regarding teachers' stress.

1   To what extent do teachers feel that they are experiencing stress?

2   What do teachers feel as the main sources of stress?

3   What are the most significant symptoms experienced?

4   Are there differences in the answers to questions?

1-3 for different biographical subgroups? Kyriacou and Sutcliffe (1978a, b) asked subjects for biographical information regarding the following:

1   Sex

2   Qualifications

3   Age

4   Length of teaching experience

5   Position held in school

The survey questions consisted of fifty-one items regarding potential sources of stress that the teacher had to rate on a 1-5 scale in response to the questions. "As a teacher how great a source of stress are these factors to you?" Approximately 20 percent of the respondents rated being a teacher as being stressful or extremely stressful.

To see if self-reported stress was associated with the biographical characteristics of these teachers, four separate two-way factorial analyses of variance was performed. All four analyses revealed significant difference. The fifty-one sources of stress were subject to a principal component analysis. The four main groups of extracted factors can be labeled as follows:

1   Pupils' behavior
2   Poor working conditions
3   Time pressure
4   Poor school ethos

Kyriacou and Sutcliffe's research indicated that female teachers found several items, including pupils' behavior to be greater sources of stress than their male colleagues. University graduates reported less stress than their colleagues on a mixture of items. These reported stresses were often in relation to working conditions and poor school ethos. Younger and less experienced teachers differed from their colleagues on a large range of items, which included greater stress in connection with punishing difficult pupils and difficult classes. Other teachers' concerns included poor promotion opportunities, lack of participation in decision making, and attitudes and behavior of the headmaster. Well over half the items were rated greater sources of stress by teachers as compared with heads of departments. Cox and Brockley (1984) state that their research, which includes reports of stress by primary and secondary teachers, suggests that teachers experienced more stress than non-teachers.

These studies on stress discussed here appear similar to stress experienced by teachers in Jamaica. It could be hypothesized, however, that teachers in Jamaica, both of primary and secondary schools, have been experiencing other stress factors in greater depth than those discussed by Kyriacou and Sutcliffe in their research mentioned earlier. It would seem appropriate then at this stage to look more closely at particular sources of teacher stress. I have selected poor working conditions and pupils' behavior which is common to both Jamaica and UK along with relationship between staff and government policies. I must add, however, that all these sources are experienced in both countries but in different degrees.

2.3   Sources of Teacher Stress

Poor Working Conditions

The environment that teachers work in is very important. Studies by Wilson and Evans (1980) found that the building themselves can have a psychological significance and the "large echoing empty spaces are equally to be avoided since in them excitement can escalate." The pupils can find the buildings depressing as the teachers do too. Harland (1975) indicates that the appearance and order of the classroom can influence pupils so often damage caused by vandalism goes unrepaired due to lack of immediate funds and the buildings are then open to further damage and a lack of respect. The physical aspect of working conditions of the school can include the following:

1   Badly constructed buildings with poor sound roofing
2   Poorly maintained buildings that are in need of constant painting and repair
3   Vandalized schools covered in graffiti or windows that have metal plates put in because the glass has been broken so many times

Dunham (1984) believes that three kinds of pressure are generated when the environment is poor. They are physical, financial, and organizational. The financial constraints are becoming increasingly significant. Dunham (1984) comments thus: "Reduced school budgets have meant low levels of expenditure on equipment and textbooks and smaller LEA funds have resulted in the re-deployment of teachers, redundancies, school closure, narrowing of promotion opportunities and the restriction of career prospects." The present financial situation and the constraints upon the teaching force cause anxiety among many teachers. The reduction in school budget has meant textbooks cannot be bought to replace the old or outdated ones. Pupils have to share more equipment, and this can lead to greater disturbance in lessen time. Teachers are frustrated by the lack of resources and become angry when schools from upper and middle class areas have Parent Teacher Associations supplementing school capitation with generous donations. The schools in the poorer areas are less fortunate.

Teachers can of course exacerbate the difficult conditions in school as reported by Gray (1985). They rebel, they become bad tempered, awkward, and unreasonable; they play truant by staying off sick or attending courses and meetings. They are late for lessons and do not prepare work or mark it. Their feelings of dissatisfaction do nothing to improve "morale" in the staffroom. As Bowers (1984) comments "Ultimately the success of a school will rest upon the effectiveness of its most vital resources—its teachers."

2.4   Relationship between Staff

A head's relationship with the staff in his/her school is both a vital part of working life and a major potential source of distress. Poor relationships can be extremely damaging to the head's work performance and ultimately the school. Quite often, teachers are not consulted over decision making in their schools. Sponou and Capoto (1979) as reported in Bowers (1984) point out that teachers "view the lack of opportunity to participate in school decision making as a major contribution of teacher's stress." Good relationships between heads and teachers can be a key factor in improving school performance and effectiveness. The old adage which says, "If a house be divided against itself, that house cannot stand," still has a ring of truth. Poor relationship breeds a climate of low trust and low supportiveness in dealing with school problems as well as generates low job satisfaction on the head.

The strain in relationship with peers is equally important, and today it is an insidious stressor in schools. Teachers may take time off school due to illness. Where such teachers have experienced marked difficulty in controlling a class, they may succumb to stress by taking time off school supposedly for colds, flu, or migraines. In time, a progression of absence leads to resentment in other staff, who have to cover the teacher's lessons. This may tend to reduce support and sympathy for the teacher on their return. This may lead to even greater strain, requiring even more time off school. When these frustrating circumstances are prolonged, depression is reported. If stress situations are not reduced, the drain in the teacher's emotional resources may lead to exhaustion, breakdown, and "burnout" (Dunham, 1983).

2.5   Government Policies

Special Needs

The Warnock Report (1978) was followed by the 1981 Education Act. This act, which amended the law to special education, brought with it much change both in special and ordinary schools. The authority must make a statement of provision which sets out the educational needs of the pupils and the arrangements to be made for their special education.

The statement must be maintained and reviewed annually. Parents have the right of access to the statement and the right to appeal against the LEA decision. Brennan (1982) explains the change and points out that requirements to fully implement the act "will make demands on expenditures." The demands placed upon the school and teachers are enormous. "Changes in teacher education are crucial," says Brennan. What Brennan did not realize in 1982 was that the government had no intention of increasing expenditure to meet the demand placed upon already stretched resources. Bookbinder (1983) commented that the act will "result in a great deal of professional time being spent in writing reports, compiling statements, and attending meetings."

In the NAS/UWT document "Education in Crisis" they give examples of some authorities figures.

Total school population	30,805
Number of full statement in special schools	215
Number of full statement in mainstream	13

In paragraph 51 it says that because the government has given little or no help to local authorities in their attempt to carry out the 1981 act, many have been left with a stark choice either to try to comply with the act with limited resources or recognize from the outset that only very modest progress can be made unless more money is made available. Most authorities put pressure on heads to conform to the regulations but no additional staffing is allowed. Shaw et al. (1981) as mentioned in Bowers (1984) reported from the US where government policy increased the demand placed upon teachers in Special Education. The authors have identified as potential stressor the change in demand as annual and other periodic review, by shifting teachers' roles from a class base to a resource orientation and by the increasing ambiguity of expectation, which results from decategorization of pupils.

In a report by Her Majesty's Inspector (1985) there is a clear warning to the government by the HMI who says that "it seems unlikely that present levels of expenditure will be sufficient to enable schools to respond successfully to the national and local calls for improvement in pupils' achievement and in the national curriculum." It is hoped the government recognizes that there is now an urgent need to assess the staffing demands of new policies and the increased calls these policies will make on teachers' time.

The educational system has changed drastically since then. There has been a change of the curriculum from decentralization to centralization. The new act altered the base power structure of the education system. It was intended to mark a radical shift in direction.

> The education system had operated for more than forty years on the basis of RA Buthler's 1944 Act, which in turn built on the Balfour Act of 1902. We need to inject a new vitality into that system. It has become producer dominated. (Mr. Bakir debate, House of Commons, December 1, 1987)

The curriculum has now been taken out of the hands of teachers. We now see the establishment of the national curriculum for five- to sixteen-year-old compulsory education. There has also been a shift from the LEA; the local management of schools can now target their own finances and spend it themselves.

This new education act in my opinion has its negative and positive sides. Teachers are now expressing the view that the budget is now limited and they stand the chance of losing their jobs easily. There is also the point that the closure of schools have been taken out of the hands of the LEA.

It is interesting to note, however, that schools are now governed by governing bodies, which makes them more democratic although at the same time they are breaking the strong influences of the school.

2.6   Pupil Behavior

I suggested earlier that pupils' behavior is a major contributory factor to teacher stress. The investigation done by Kyriacou and Sutcliffe (1978a, b) would appear to support this view. Dunham (1981) highlighted pupils' behavior to be a major contributory factor to teachers' stress. Pupils' misbehavior is often termed as being "disruptive." Disruptive behavior is an ambiguous description, which can include noisy, overactive children to abusive, insolent, and violent pupils. Dunham (1981) cites the survey carried out by Clwyd County Education Department (1976), where disruptive behavior was analyzed into six categories:

1   Damage to property

2   Rowdiness

3   Actual violence

4   Threats to violence

5   Sexual misbehavior

6   Theft

The survey concluded that the greatest problem was "rowdiness," which included deliberate lateness for lessons, pupils' disturbance in the lesson and verbal abuse, and refusal to cooperate. This kind of behavior is escalating in Jamaica and is more evident in the secondary schools.

The teachers' aim to establish and maintain order, in order to teach, should always be strived for. This battle for order between teacher and pupil has always existed and is far removed from the strong emotions expressed by some pupils against their teachers. Lloyd Smith (1984) points to the present economic situation in the UK as a reason for disruptive behavior. A parallel could be drawn from here with the Jamaica's economic situation, which is a grave concern where students are concerned. The prospect of unemployment which faced more and more older school children could, it might be hypothesized, have had a direct effect on their attitudes to schooling and their responses to authority and control in school.

The reasons for disruptive behavior, it appears, are numerous. The effects upon the teaching force are equally varied. Dunham (1984) sees the interaction between disruptive pupil behavior and stress in teaching as a "two-way process: the former can be either a cause or an effect of the latter."

Further research has suggested that relationships between teachers within schools are of major importance and that hostility and lack of rapport between teachers or teachers and heads can influence the environment for pupils in such a way that disruption becomes a likely consequence. In particular, a lack of consensus regarding the "approach to management" can lead to major inconsistence in "toleration limits," with the result that quite different expectations regarding behavior are transmitted to the pupils. Serious inconsistencies between teachers may promote a chaotic situation with pupils confused and liable to exploit the lack of consensus and teacher's solidarity.

It is possible to analyze disruption from many different stand points. For a thorough analysis, it is necessary to consider all factors relating to the particular individuals (pupils and teachers), to interaction and social structure within the classroom, to factors in school organization and ethos, and to educational policy and the wider social context. It is likely that the interactions between elements from these different levels is amazingly complex and need to involve interdisciplinary thinking. At present, work/studies in the area derive from several alterative perspectives and results many seem contradictory. However, it cannot be doubted that many quite different approaches may offer more useful information to help understand this phenomenon of disruption.

It seems, therefore, that there are many sources of stress for teachers, which can be both frequent and intense. Kyriacou and Sutcliffe (1978a, b) split these sources into four categories as mentioned before. Before looking at the manifestation of stress, I think it is important to look first at the term "burnout" and how it is associated with teacher stress.

2.7   Teacher Burnout

The use of the term "burnout" is popularly associated with stress research in North America and, in particular, with the work conducted by Christina Maslach. She highlights the wide variance of expert opinion as to the exact meaning of the term. Maslach and Jackson (1981) suggest that people who are labeled as suffering from "burnout" share the following occupational pattern. "People involved in prolonged, constant, intensive interaction with people in an emotionally charged atmosphere are susceptible to the syndrome of burnout" (Schwab, 1983: 21). Maslach and Jackson (1981) point out that the component parts of burnout include the following:

1   Emotional exhaustion
2   Negative attitudes to clients
3   Loss of feeling of accomplishment on the job

Spaniol and Caputo (1978) have identified three levels of burnout:

1   First-degree burn which they term as mild, which often includes short bouts of irritation, fatigue, worry, and frustration.
2   Second-degree burn, which is termed as moderate similar in characteristics as mild but lasts for two to three weeks at a time.
3   Third-degree burn termed severe when the sufferer has to contend with ailments, such as ulcers, chronic back pain, and migraine headaches, etc

As a result of intensive action over a prolonged period of time, a teacher's emotional energies are drained. The teacher is aware that he cannot extend himself as in earlier years in relationship to his students; in some cases this may be accompanied by negative attitudes that he may transmit toward his pupils in overt ways, such as being sarcastic or derogatory. Caution is required here as some people may be perceived as sarcastic, and this may be considered to be an enduring trait of their personality, rather than a direct result of their suffering from burnout.

In education, it is assumed that teachers do not enter the occupation solely for financial rewards. It is thought that they are motivated or "called" because they can and want to help pupils to develop their potential. Therefore, if a teacher has no feeling of accomplishment in performing certain aspects of his task, this will have important consequences for both pupil and teacher.

The term "burnout" as used by Maslach and Jackson is used as a general term to describe the feelings of people in the helping profession who find that the stress involved with their work environment has altered their original feelings about themselves and their work. Suffering from burnout may have consequences that would affect

1   other colleagues; this may be termed as "negative conditioning";
2   students; and
3   the reputation of the institution.

Maslach and Jackson (1981) point out that their research indicates that teachers who experience burnout are more likely to

1   leave their job;
2   report sick;
3   increase their input of alcohol; or
4   have family and marital conflict.

As all teachers are involved in similar activities, this raises the question as to why some teachers exhibit feelings of burnout and others do not. Research findings of Schwab and Inawaki (1980) may provide part of the answer. They studied 479 randomly selected teachers from Massachusetts. Their findings suggested that there were certain relevant personal and background variables and that these were related to levels of teacher burnout. It is of interest that teachers did not differ in their feelings of burnout when classified according to

1   teaching experience (years);
2   experience in urban/suburban or rural schools;
3   family details;
4   marital status; and
5   degree status—trained/graduate, etc.

In contrast, they did differ on why they were grouped according to sex, grade level taught, and age. Age was found to be an important factor in feelings of emotional exhaustion and tiredness. Young teachers had more intense feelings than others. This may be related to lack of experience and, therefore, less-sophisticated coping strategies.

Sex and grade level related to teachers' feelings of depersonalization. Male teachers were found to have more negative feelings or attitudes toward students than females. This may be a reaction to the reduction of occupational choice which males face compared to females. The latter may exercise choice as to whether or not they continue to work in teaching after child rearing. High schools and junior high schools were more negative than elementary school teachers.

In conclusion, it is obvious that the recognition of the symptom "burnout" is a useful tool in understanding more about teachers' stress as we proceed to look at its manifestation.

2.8   Manifestation of Stress

Studies indicate three major categories of stress manifestation: these being emotional, behavioral, and physiological. Typically symptoms of stress, which are also manifestations, are those physiologically related indications of poor mental health; manifestations of stress, as used in general discourse, more often refer to adverse emotional and behavioral changes in the individual. For the purpose of the present discussion, all three are considered manifestations of stress. It appears usual for manifestation to interact with one or another differently across time. For example, one of the most pronounced manifestations of stress is the amount of time involved in trying to maintain some kind of order. This manifestation was noted by Fuller (1979) in his research. He noted that when teachers are placed in stressful situations, their priorities change. In order of importance, these become (a) survival training, (b) classroom performance, (c) methods on how to make an impact on students, and (d) concern about increasing what pupils learn. Interestingly, under less stressful situations or conditions, these priorities become reversed, with concern for students receiving first priority.

Another common manifestation of stress is that of excessive worry, particularly, the anxious, anticipatory kind. Here the individual spends more time worrying about the likelihood of events in the future rather than what is happening in the present. Hebb (1972) suggested that a slight degree of anxiety could be stimulating and energizing, but that higher levels of anxiety, produced through increasing demands, could prove unproductive in the sense that the teacher's ability to make practical or realistic decisions is impaired. As a result, Hebb considered that confusion, panic, exhaustion, and nervous breakdown may follow. In addition, processes are affected, which, in turn, affects behavior and performance. This may lead to physiological changes, such as accelerated heart rate, rapid breathing, and perspiration. The relationship between anxiety and the teacher's performance or his or her task is summarized in figure 4. Between the amount of time spent "holding things together" and worrying, less and less teaching occurs.

Koon (1971) observed that high-anxiety teachers used significantly fewer task-orientated behavior with pupils and tended to administer fewer reinforcing consequences. An instructor article in 1979 concluded that teachers may be so concerned with their own well-being that little time is left for teaching and other professional concerns.

Keifaber and Katzentein (1979) identified the following as manifestations of excessively stressed, or as they put it "professionally burned out," teachers: excessive use of derogatory, demeaning, or abstract terminology; dealing with student on only intellectual levels; total separation of job life from personal life; hiding behind impersonal bureaucratic rules; physiological distancing; excessive use of "sick humor"; physical and or physiological abuse of others; and excessive use of drugs, e.g. tranquillizers and alcohol.

Figure 4: The Relationship between Increasing Demands and the Performance of the Teachers' Tasks.

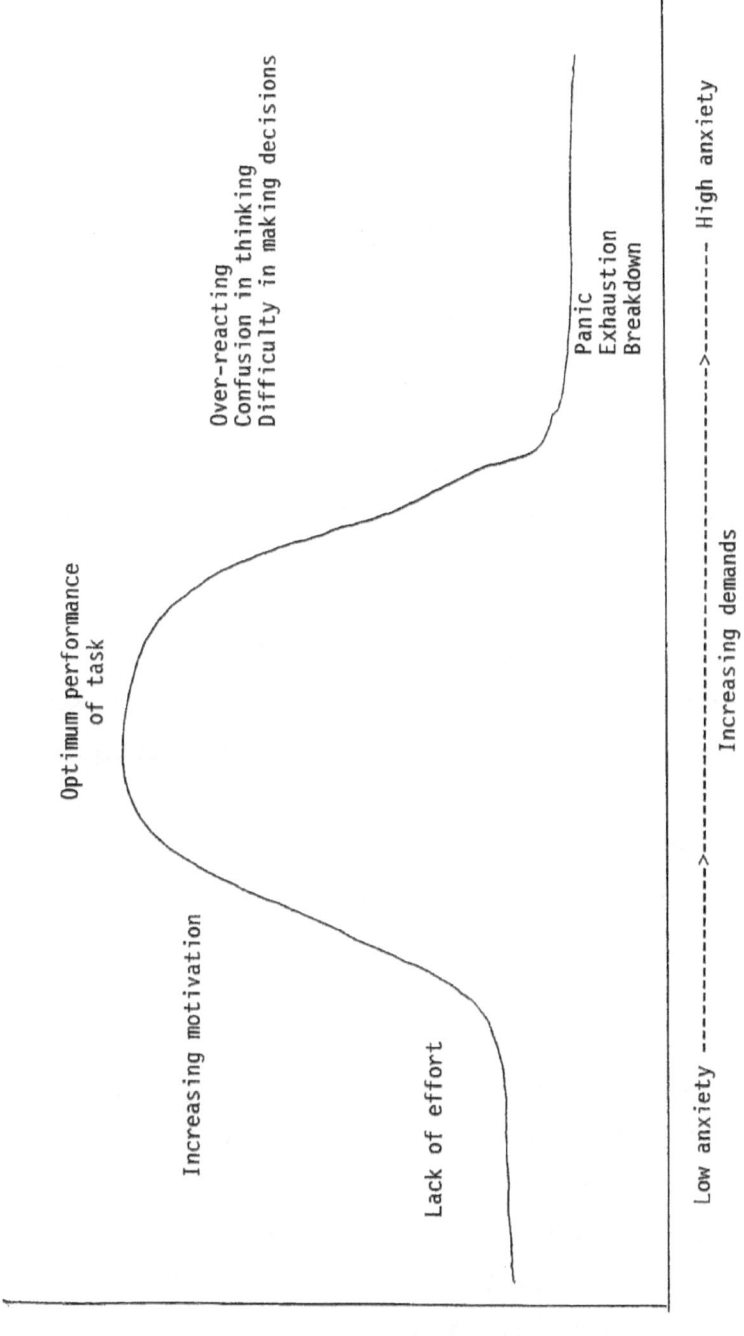

In an Instructor survey (1972) in the UK, which asked if health hazards were related to teaching, 84 percent of the 7,000 teacher respondents answered with a definite "yes." The connection between one's mental and physical well-being or health have been the subjects of hypotheses since Plate's era; even in this present age, evidence is still being gathered in support of this theory. The common symptoms of British teachers under stress, as reported by Kyriacou and Sutcliffe (1978a, b), included exhaustion, frustration, and an awareness of stress symptoms, usually manifested as their being "very tense." The 1972 Instructor survey reported more specific symptoms, namely, migraine and sinus headaches; allergies; colds; postnasal drip; hypertension; bladder, kidney, and bowel problems; colitis; "nervous stomach"; acne; and overweight. In both studies, all symptoms were described as occurring frequently.

Cohen (1978) noted other physiological changes: these being, stress-induced hormonal changes that alter the organ system in the body; stress-induced sudden death; temporary by frequent elevation of blood pressure, placing strain on the heart and subsequently leading to chronic hypertension; the release of toxins stored in the body tissue; and possible contribution of stress to cancer. These findings give support to those of Bloch's (1978): i.e., gastrointestinal disorders (burning sensation, cramping, nausea, diarrhea, ulcers, colitis); musculoskeletal disorders (backaches); respiratory disorders (asthma, frequent bronchial infections); headaches (migraines, tension); cardiovascular disorders (palpitations, hypertension, coronary artery disease, and atherosclerosis); and various other manifestations, including "combat" neuroses, emotional tension, anxiety, insecurity, nightmares, excessive startle responses, phobias, cognitive impairment, conversion symptoms, weakness, blurred vision, "malaise" despondency and other so-called "depressive equivalents." Many of the symptoms mentioned in these studies are also found in nonstressful situations; however, their frequency under stressful conditions was found to be significantly above that which would be otherwise expected.

Assuming that each individual defines his or her own reactions to stress according to particular situations and personal variables, knowing the sources and manifestations should enable the teacher to enact more effectively to one of the number of stress-reduction techniques.

Chapter 3

Methods and Administrative Procedure

3.1   Method

From the discussion of the models of teacher stress in chapter 1, it is apparent that the perception of the teachers in the stress situation is very important in determining whether one is under stress. This emphasis on subjective appraisal of one's circumstances has brought investigators to the assumption that teachers are able to provide valid reports of causes of experienced stress, or their reaction. This self-reported approach has proven very successful in studies elsewhere (Cherry, 1978; Dunham, 1976, 1980; Kyriacou and Sutcliffe, 1977, 1978a, b, 1980).

The national survey of Health and Development (Cherry, 1978) and the National Education Association in the United States (reported by Coates and Thoresen, 1976) have used a format of questionnaire with single item to measure teacher stress and have proven to be most successful. Nonetheless, Kyriacou (1977) argues that it has a shortcoming of failure to take into account the fact that different teachers may interpret the meaning to be affected by ego-defensive processes and that teachers may genuinely lack insight into their situation. It has its own practical advantages.

Questionnaires, according to Tall (1988), are a rapid and confidential means of collecting a large number of detailed views. They can be mailed or handed to respondents, and the respondents have time to consider the questions before answering. The main advantage is not that it is easy to use but also that it is a more general measure of stress rather than a measure at a particular moment. Besides, it can be used as an index of the prevalence of teacher stress, and of the proportion experiencing a great deal of stress compared with those experiencing little stress.

The disadvantages however, are that the response rate may be low and respondents may not understand the question. Nachimas and Nachimas (1981) give the response rate of mail survey as between 20 and 40 percent as against 95 percent for personal interviews. Survey researchers who use mail questionnaires have always dealt with the problems of how to estimate the effect that non-respondents may have on their findings.

To identify the main causes of teachers stress, reaction to stress and coping strategies, investigators like Dunham (1980), Kyriacou and Sutcliffe (1978a) have used the self-reported rating method which proved to be more successful. Considering the success of these researchers, the writer is convinced that the self-report approach—a questionnaire with single items for rating or to choose—is suitable to achieve the aim of this study.

The questionnaire consisted of three parts: the first part comprises of background questions and the second and third parts are the checklists. The first ten questions requested biographical information regarding sex, length of teaching, qualification, etc. The second section asked about causes of stress and consisted of sixteen items derived from Kyriacou and Sutcliffe's (1978a, b) checklists. The third section consisted of twenty-eight items taken form Dunham's (1980) checklist. Teachers were asked to tick the reactions they had felt to stress over this year. These questionnaires were chosen because the researcher could identify their relevance to the Jamaican situation and also for the benefit of the comparison that the study wishes to draw.

3.2   Administrative Procedure

The study is confined to schools taken from the rural and urban areas in Jamaica. There are a total of five schools, all of which are secondary schools. Five schools were chosen because the writer needed to get a cross section of responses. These schools were taken from the urban and rural areas in Jamaica and were chosen specifically because of their location and organization. In order to ensure that the findings reflected as general a picture as possible, the writer attempted to send the questionnaires to at least thirty teachers who worked in these five schools.

Before the study, a request was made through a colleague of mine to the five schools that were chosen to seek permission for the administration of the questionnaire in their schools. A sample questionnaire was sent to my colleague by mail, who then made 150 copies directed by me, and a cover letter, explaining the purpose of these questionnaires (see Appendix I). These were distributed to thirty teachers in all five schools selected. These questionnaires were returned to me personally by someone traveling from Jamaica to the UK. There was no long delay in receiving these questionnaires from my colleague, and from corresponding with my colleague in Jamaica, the only problem experienced was that respondents did not return all the questionnaires at the time specified. One colleague, however, in the school I had worked in before coming to England sent to say that these questionnaires had generated a discussion amongst staff in the staffroom. They actually had not looked at their problem as being a result of stress. I was somewhat happy to hear this because one of my reasons for undertaking this particular research was my knowledge of the fact that stress has never been an issue in our Jamaican Educational System.

One hundred and twenty seven questionnaires were returned. This represents 84.6 percent of the sample. The response is quite satisfactory taking into consideration that, at the time of administration, teachers were busy preparing for end-of-year examinations and had a lot of work to do.

However, the use of checklists to obtain information in Jamaica about staff reaction to occupational pressures has several disadvantages. Perhaps the worst is that some questions are probably understood differently. Another problem may be that teachers experiencing stress may not want to reveal the full extent of this, either to themselves or to others, even confidentially, especially in Jamaica where, as I stated before, this topic is not presently an issue.

This could mean that they have engaged in some sort of ego-defense mechanism, or simply that they lack insight into their own situation. Also, the checklists returned showed that not all the teachers in each school completed and returned questionnaires. The analysis of replies is restricted to those who had given answers to the questionnaires. Chapter 4 now goes on to show results and analysis of the research done.

Chapter 4

Results and Discussion

Out of the original sample of 150 teachers, thirty from each of the five schools, 127 questionnaires were returned; i.e., a return percentage of 84.6 percent.

Of the 127 that were returned, four were inadequately completed in that Part III was left unanswered. A copy of section 1 is included.

4.1 Section I: Concerning Gender, Years of Service, Qualifications, and In-service Work

Question 1.1   Gender
There were ninety-five females and thirty-two males. This is not unusual. The population of female teachers in Jamaica is always greater than males.

Question 1.2   Teaching Experience
This shows 32.3 percent of the sample has teaching experiences between 0-5 years while 14.5 percent has between 16-20 years, although not all at the same place.

Question 1.3   Position Held
Although not deliberately engineered, the sample proved to be a representative mixture of staff, varying from principals to junior

teachers with the latter having the greatest percentage, i.e. 38.6 percent.

Question 1.4   Time in Present Position

55.9 percent of the sample had been in their current post between 0-5 years, 22 percent had been in post between 6-10 years, while 2.5 percent had been in post for twenty-one years or over.

Questions 1.5 and 1.6   Level of Qualification

The level of qualification ranged from

	%
Diploma	50.9
Others	31.0
Teacher training	11.2
PGCE	6.9

Question 1.7   Area of Training

The majority had specially trained in secondary and primary education. Only six had higher education and one special education. Sixteen did not respond to the question.

	%
Secondary education	46.8
Primary education	46.8
Higher education	5.4
Missing	.9%

Question 1.8   Adequacy of Training in Relation to the Management of Children

The response to this section shows that the bulk of teachers found the training very or reasonably adequate. There was little dissatisfaction with classroom management training, perhaps because discipline in Jamaican schools is perceived as more controlled than in the UK.

	%
Completely adequate	7.9
Very adequate	30.8
Reasonably adequate	59
Not very adequate	6.8
Not sure	3.4
Please specify	0

Question 1.9   Coping Strategies

In this section, some teachers felt that the knowledge of school policies and the acquisition of personal skills would make them better able to cope. However, the large majority thought neither of the above would help.

	%
Personal skills	9.7
School policies	12.6
Neither of the above	67.7

Questionnaire Paper I

Please tick and insert appropriate answers unless otherwise specified:

1. Gender   Male 32 26.8   Female 95 73.2
2. Teaching   0-5   40 32.3   6-10   24 19.24
   Experience 11-15 21 16.9   16-20 18 14.5
   21 and   16.9
   Over 21

3. Please state position held in school

	No.	%
Principal	5	5
Vice principal	6	5.9
Senior teacher	38	37.6
PE teacher	2	2.0
Junior teacher	49	38.6
Business education	1	1.0
Others	26	20.5

4. Number of years in present position:

	No.	%
0-5	66	55.9
6-10	26	22.0
11-15	12	10.2
16-20	11	9.3
21 and over 21	3	2.5

5. Level of qualification:

		%
Teacher training	13	11.2
Diploma	59	50.9
PGCE	8	6.9
Other	36	31.0

6. If answer to Question 5 was "other," please specify.

Other   36   31.0%

7. My training was in

	No.	%
Primary education	52	46.8
Secondary education	52	46.8
Special education	1	.9
Higher education	6	5.4
Missing	16	12.6

8. Please specify what sort of in-service courses or upgrading courses teachers in your school are currently undergoing:

	No.	%
One year upgrading	20	5
Certificate qualification		
Diploma qualification	10	10

9. Do you consider the initial training you received in terms of dealing with students as

	No.	%
Very adequate	36	30.8
Reasonably adequate	69	59.0

Not sure	4	3.4
Not very adequate	8	6.8
Completely adequate	10	7.9
Please specify	0	0

10. What would make you feel better able to cope with incidents involving conflicts either with students or staff?

		%
Personal skills	25	9.7
School policies	16	12.6
None	86	67.7

4.2   Section II

The results of the first checklist indicate that the frequency of causes associated with stress were as follows:

Rank order	Description	No. of responses
1	Lack of facilities	99
2	Attitude of students	88
3	Salary received	73
4	Lack of resources	69
5	Attitudes of teachers	46

Lack of facilities is found to be the major cause of teachers' stress for both male and female in all five schools. There were no significant sex differences in perception of causes of stress.

This section below shows the comparison between rural and urban schools using the causes shown above.

Causes of Stress in Order of Magnitude

Description	Position in rural schools	Position in urban schools
	No. of teachers	No. of teachers
1 Lack of facilities	65	34
2 Attitude of students	38	50
3 Salary received	50	23
4 Lack of resources	50	19
5 Attitude to teachers	21	25

Table 1: Results

	Causes of stress	No. of mentions	% teachers
1.	Lack of facilities	99	78
2.	Attitude of students	88	69.3
3.	Salary received	73	57.5
4.	Lack of resources	69	54.3
5.	Attitude of teachers	46	36.2
6.	School buildings	43	33.9
7.	Bureaucracy	41	32.3
8.	Absenteeism of colleagues	37	21.1
9.	Parents	36	28.3
10.	School organization	32	25.2
11.	Conflicts between home and work demands	16	12.6
12.	Excessive number of meetings	15	11.8
13.	Duties	13	10.2
14.	Position held	13	10.2
15.	Advisors	10	7.9
16.	Others	8	6.3

There is no agreement between (can't read) stress response in the schools of both rural and (can't read) (as shown above). Lack of facilities which shows ninety-nine teachers from both areas seeing this as the most obvious cause of stress had the greater number in the rural areas. Schools in the rural areas, from the chart shows, experience greater stress in all areas except salary received and attitude to teachers.

4.3   Lack of Facilities

In Jamaica the Ministry in charge of Education has always placed more emphasis on schools which are located in the urban areas. These schools are located in what we commonly call the town areas where tourists and other visitors are always visiting. There has always been the effort to keep these schools in very good conditions, good, clean structures, and adequate facilities for both teachers and students.

The common entrance examination which is administered to 11 + annually in Jamaica has its greatest percentage passes from schools in the urban areas since its inception. The argument put forward by concerned parents at a Parent Teachers Association meeting held at the school I was working at in Jamaica was that their children in the rural or country areas are at a disadvantage as the government does not make adequate provision for them.

4.4   Attitude to Students

Teachers' attitude to students has been a reaction of frustration over the years. Teachers are angry because of the conditions in which they have to work and the criticisms they receive when students do not achieve academically.

4.5   Salary Received

A lot cannot be said about salary received except for the continuous call of teachers to the government that the salary they are receiving is much too small for what the job entails. Although teachers are paid according to their qualifications, they are not able to maintain a high standard of living due to economic inflation in Jamaica. The urban schools perceived less than half the stress of the rural schools because teachers with high qualifications normally find jobs in the urban schools, where promotion to senior teacher, etc. is most likely.

4.6   Lack of Resources

The lack of resources as a greater cause of stress in the rural schools are subjected to things mentioned in the discussion of lack of facilities. Other contributory factors are very bad roads for transportation to travel to make deliveries to the schools, lack of electricity to enhance subjects, such as science, chemistry, etc. and well-trained and experienced teachers refuse to live in some remote parts of the country. This results in the school being unable to cope without good resources to enhance its educational success.

4.7   Attitude to Teachers

There is no marked difference in the attitude to teachers, but evidently it has been ranked number 5 in causes of stress. We could conclude therefore that schools in both areas have seen this as a great cause of stress.

4.8   Discussion

From table 1, which shows the results of the causes of stress experienced by teachers in both areas, it must be noted that there are other areas that have been seen as causes of stress. For example, a great number of teachers cited school buildings, bureaucracy, and absenteeism of colleagues, parents, and school organization as causes of stress. All these can be argued from the point that the Ministry in charge of Education need to put more emphasis on the whole organization of school policies and administration.

There were other areas, however, which were not seen as great causes of stress. Teachers seem to cope well with the number of meetings they have to attend and the duties they have to perform. Teachers in Jamaica are quite happy to perform duties that are not intrinsic to the job as was discussed earlier in this study. It is also clear that teachers do not see the position they hold in school as a great cause of stress. Positions held in schools are usually given to teachers with most experience and also their level of qualifications.

4.9   Comparison with the United Kingdom

Kyriacou and Sutcliffe (1978a, b) (from which my checklist was taken) administered a four-section questionnaire to 257 teachers, one section which consists of fifty-seven items regarding sources of teachers' stress on a five-point scale (no stress to extreme stress).

The data from the fifty-seven sources of stress was subjected to factor analysis, and four factors were extracted. These were labeled as follows:

Description	No.	%
Pupils' behavior	1	18.6
Poor working conditions	2	12.2
Time pressure	3	11.9
Poor school ethos	4	9.3

The first five variables that were ranked highest in Jamaica were not fully comparable to that of Kyriacou and Sutcliffe, except behavior is ranked No. 1 on their list whereas attitude of students which is comparable to pupils' behavior is ranked No. 2 in Jamaica. Second, lack of facilities which is ranked No. 5 in Jamaica and can be compared to poor working conditions is ranked No. 2 in the UK.

These are only two obvious similarities here between the two countries where these two causes are concerned. The other causes in both countries are different. In general, the pattern of the two analyses shows that Jamaica, being a less developed country in terms of resources and facilities, the nature of the school, the pupils involved, and its culture on a whole, is different to that of the UK, which has more facilities and resources to offer its students. Teachers in the UK are also better paid than teachers in Jamaica.

4.10 Section III

The result of this questionnaire indicated that the most frequently mentioned reactions to stress were as follows:

Description	No.	%
Frustration	1	53.5
Moodiness	2	44.1
Feeling of exhaustion	3	38.6
Tension headaches	4	37.0
Wanting to leave teaching	5	36.2

In comparison with Dunham (1983) on which my checklist was based, he administered his checklist in 1982 and 1983 in three comprehensive schools that he had been invited to work in. In his work, the teachers were asked to indicate which reactions they had experienced in the present school year, and a rough assessment of their frequency was sought by asking them to identify which they have experienced very often, often, sometimes, or rarely. I, however, asked the teachers to tick any of the following reactions to work stress they had experienced over the year. A copy is shown overleaf.

Dunham chose the first five highest reactions teachers had to stress; these were as follows:

Description	No.	%
Frustration	7	55
Feeling of exhaustion	8	55
Tension headaches	6	35
Disturbed sleep	13	73
Withdrawal from staff contact	9	56

Table 2: Reaction to Stress

	No.	%
Frustration	68	53.5
Moodiness	56	44.1
Feeling of exhaustion	49	38.6
Tension headaches	47	37.0
Wanting to leave teaching	46	36.2
Anger	26	20.5
Depression	39	30.7
Feeling of being unable to cope	32	25.2
Anxiety	26	20.5
Irritability	23	18.1
Absenteeism	12	9.4
Disturbed sleep	20	15.7
Inability to make decisions	15	11.8
Uncomfortable confrontation with parents	14	11.0
Poor concentration	12	9.4
Marked reduction of contact with pupils outside school	10	9.9
Displaced, aggression, displacement on to children, colleagues or pupils outside school	9.9	7.2
Apathy	9	7.1
Unwilling to support colleagues	9	7.1
Withdrawal from staff contact	8	6.3
Feeling of isolation in school	8	6.3
Increased eating	7	5.5
Feeling of fear	6	4.7
Skin rash	5	3.9
Feeling of guilt	5	3.9
Increased smoking	3	2.4
Feeling of inferiority	2	1.6
Increased drinking	2	1.6

4.11 Comparison with Jamaica and the United Kingdom

Frustration came first on both lists. Teachers in Jamaica and UK experience similar first reaction to stress. So evidently frustration is a common reaction to stress to teachers in general of both countries.

4.12 Feeling of Exhaustion and Tension Headaches

Feelings of exhaustion and tension headaches also appear on both lists, although "exhaustion" is marked by the highest number of UK researchers. The similarity here is that they both appear in the first five that are ranked highest in both countries.

4.13 Moodiness

In the Jamaican result moodiness appears second. Jamaican teachers from my experience usually have this reaction whenever they become uncomfortable. It is probably a worldwide reaction and is associated with the Jamaican culture, where this is a normal reaction to stress which comes in any situation.

4.14 Wanting to Leave Teaching

Wanting to leave teaching was ranked five on the Jamaican result. It did not appear on Dunham's list. I wonder if the low morale in the teaching profession due to salary, working conditions, and lack of resources which I fared when I was in Jamaica has any bearing at present on the fact that 36.2% reported wanting to leave teaching.

In Dunham's (1984) results

School A reported 25%
School B reported 15%
School C reported 20%

This gives an average of 20%, which is less than the percentage given for Jamaica.

4.15 Disturbed Sleep

Disturbed sleep was ranked fourth on Dunham's list but did not appear at all in the Jamaican first five; it appeared twelfth on the Jamaica list with 15.7 percent. This shows that teachers in the UK are more emotionally affected by stress than Jamaican teachers. Jamaican teachers, if they are in the urban areas, have a lot to occupy their time; after a full day of teaching, they would go out to other social activities, which at the end of the day makes them very tired and susceptible to a good night's sleep. Teachers in the rural area, however, have very little to do after work and so they generally look forward to an early night at home. The point I would make from Dunham's findings is that teachers in the UK are too restricted in their control of the students that they have to teach, and this affects them mentally and results in disturbed sleep, whereas in Jamaica teachers are allowed to discipline students accordingly.

4.16 Withdrawal from Staff Contact

Withdrawal from staff contact appeared fifth on Dunham's list, but on the Jamaican list, it was number twenty with 6.3 percent. This shows a marked difference between both countries. Teaching in Jamaica has always been seen as a high-profile job; in this respect, teachers always give moral support to each other in any situation which may arise.

4.17 Discussion

The findings of the present study indicate that over 80 percent of respondents in Jamaica found a number of causes being the result of the stress they are experiencing, and they also experience a number of reactions to stress. There are similarities with the research done in the UK. The differences that have been found may be partly due to cultural differences. Jamaican teachers are very reserved in expressing their views about their job to some extent. This is one of the reasons why there was such a low response to some questions that were asked.

Another reason for the low response to some questions is that the issue of stress in the teaching profession has never been researched in Jamaica, which makes teachers unaware of some of the causes of stress and their reaction to it.

Second, 40 out of 127 respondents (32.3 percent) had only five years experience, this being the highest, and forty-nine (38.6 percent) being junior teachers. Added to that fifty-nine respondents (50.9 percent) are diploma trained teachers. This diploma qualification has only been introduced into the teachers' colleges in 1985. These responses suggest that we have more young teachers in the teaching profession who are not aware of the killer disease "stress."

The present study indicates that the major causes of stress are lack of facilities, salary received, lack of resources, and attitude of teachers.

The major reactions to stress are frustration, moodiness, feeling of exhaustion, tension headaches, and wanting to leave teaching.

The difference between both countries is not great. The hypotheses proposed were as follows:

1   Stress is common to every teacher in one school or another.
2   Teachers in the UK now perceive greater stress than teachers in Jamaica.
3   Teachers experience stress for different reasons.
4   The occurrence of stress has a negative effect of teaching.

The findings tell us that stress is common to every teacher in one school or another from research done in the UK (Kyriacou and Sutcliffe, 1978a, b). Dunham (1984) compared it with the research done in Jamaica; the indication is that there is the presence of teacher stress in schools, which needs to be looked into.

It would seem, however, that teachers in the UK do not necessarily perceive greater stress than teachers in Jamaica but are able to deal more positively with the problems as they are fully aware of its existence and the damages that can result if such a problem is ignored.

Presently, teacher-training colleges are lacking systematic training in classroom-management skills and understanding of their commitment to the job, not to mention the nature of stress during professional years for student teachers, and schools are also lacking orientation programs for new teachers.

It is recommended that school organization should examine those factors so as to reduce their contribution to the existence of stress factor.

The study also indicates that the young and less-experienced teachers are greater in number and would definitely suffer more stress since they did not have skills nor experience. They are more likely to be frustrated by the enormous demands placed on them. On the other hand, their eagerness and willingness to do good and to offer help would have exerted more pressure to these new teachers. Under such conditions, it is no wonder that the young feel frustrated; many of them feel anxious because of little sense of achievement and a strong feeling to cope. Under such stress levels most young teachers are prone to illness and absence than old and experienced teachers. Such findings support work elsewhere (Kyrlacou, 1980a).

It is also suggested that stress at work may affect health since 17.3 percent of respondents reported that they were absent at some time from school during the school year. Added to that 30.7 percent of respondents were having feelings of depression, 18.1 percent became irritable, and 25.2 percent had the feeling of being unable to cope.

The investigation, although constrained by limitations of book sources in Jamaica, the research provides a general picture of teacher stress in that country and certainly the hypotheses although not greatly proved. The research has shown commonality in Jamaica and the UK. Nevertheless, it is only one of the pioneer works in Jamaica. It is hoped to call attention to this problem.

Chapter 5

Summary and Conclusions

5.1 Summary

It has been suggested that a deleterious degree of stress is inevitable at present in the teaching profession. Stress, as defined here, is the state which results from an individual assessment of demands make on one, the personal resource to cope, and the available support and constraints which exist to supplement or inhibit personal coping. When resources do not meet demand stress, is experienced.

Stress has been described as having a cognitive physiological and environmental aetiology, which results in physical symptoms being experienced. In turn, these physical manifestations of stress affect staff, reducing levels of commitment, enthusiasm and creativity, limiting openness and empathy toward students and teachers. An emotional withdrawing may be expressed physically with days off work. As tolerance and problem-solving capacities recede, teachers find work stress encroaches on their home life, impairing relationships, and reducing the potentially buffering effect they may have.

The findings in earlier chapters indicates that concern over teacher stress have been growing in the last decades, elevating the subject from "pop psychology" to accredited research. Statistics show that although stress is evident throughout the occupational spectrum, particular facets of work experience have been recognized as likely to increase the incidence of stress (MacKay and Cox, 1979). Conflicts which are inherent in the work task or within the workforce, physical risk or perceived threat, which may be integral to the nature of the work or an inevitable consequence of it (such as risk of violence from students or parents), frustrating, repetitive or monotonous work, have all been cited as stress inducers.

It can be seen that attitudes to work have changed. Theoretical models have improved our understanding of what motivates people to work. The role of financial remuneration and other rewards, stimulations, and challenges have also been illuminated. Theoretical models also disseminate information about how autonomy, control and communication influence the individual as does personal psychology, the structure and operation of the organization and the many systems with it.

A number of models of stress were explored as tools to facilitate understanding of the complex interactions of teachers and work environment. A medical approach was seen to be limited, offering a treatment-orientated model which concentrated on physical symptoms rather than on the physiological reaction as defined by Selye. Symptomatic treatment concentrating on anxiolytics and tranquillizers identifies personal dysfunction without regard to environmental influences.

The Marxist model was found to be useful, with its emphasis on the workers' perception of themselves within the work situation being influenced by good communication policies, which promote worker involvement and feeling of belonging and reduce isolation estrangement.

An ecological model offering a biological analogy illustrated the need for balanced, individual, and environmental approach to stress to fully understand the complex interactions in operation and to guide ameliorative moves. Finally, a transactional model was included, simplifying the structure of personal cognitive appraisals, stress experience, and coping activities which follow. This is a useful model for assessing and planning personal coping strategies and equally useful for assessing and planning organizational structures to facilitate coping (figure 3).

Much stress literature exists in the UK but not in Jamaica although quantifiable empirical work is limited and a diversity of data collection and interpretation generates confusion and restrict conclusive statements. Longitudinal studies do not exist to offer recommendations, which have been found to be effective. However, in comparison of recent studies of other professional occupations, stress varied according to the different settings and personal-coping skills, but major factors were defined as tasks and work features, which were inherent in the occupation being studied. Research studies in the UK located stress not only in the personality of the individual but also in the teacher/student relationship, teachers and heads and the school organization, its administrative style, school size, low salary, stability, and communication. The teachers' workload, teachers' absenteeism, lack of facilities, poor school ethos, and resources, which effectively reduce personal efficacy and standards, are also cited as causative factors. These and other major studies emphasized conflict, threat, frustration as the basis for interpersonal, personal, and structural causes of stress.

A brief examination of the changes and developments in the teaching profession in Jamaica reveals a constantly shifting scene. Government politics change along with training and examinations. Teachers are no longer allowed to enter the profession with five subjects in the Jamaica School Certificate; instead, they are required to have four General Certificate in Education O levels, including Mathematics and English and be trained for three years. Failing this, they are allowed to spend one year in college to gain the entry requirements. On successful completion, they are granted space to continue their studies for teacher qualifications (a total of four years). This is not experienced as an evolutionary process but one that ebbs and flows with the vagaries of changing government and finance.

Public acceptance and accountability has become increasingly vulnerable to media influences as teachers are reprimanded, now for taking too much action, and then for not intervening enough. Critics call for more in-depth training in basic skills, but the government has not yet responded to this call. Teachers continue to work within an atmosphere that is unsatisfactory to them.

The skills, values, and attitudes that frequently lead people into the teaching profession are also those most necessary for students' growth and achievement. Respect, positive regard, and openness also make teachers vulnerable to emotional overload. Turning to the school setting to see how powerful emotions such as these are embraced. Teachers in rural areas with less qualification than those in urban areas experience poor working conditions and low salaries, barely commensurate with the expectations, responsibilities and discretion inherent in their work. Examination loads are heavy and frequently upgrading prospects for advancements are poor, considering at that time there was only one university in Jamaica.

The organizational policies, ethos, and values have a great effect on teachers and their work. Their self-esteem identities and satisfaction are also influenced. Relationships within and beyond the school organization tend to be fraught with assumption, stereotyped misperception, and expectations, which generate insecurities and hostility.

The role of the heads as a preventative and ameliorative one is seen as crucial. Inadequate attention to the selection and training of senior teachers results in unsupported staff and stress line heads. The use of imaginative support within the school, such as special interest or teacher group support have been described as valuable, both for the prevention of stress and for the individual development of the teaching staff.

Professional- and post-qualifying training have been described as a major instrument for the preparation of teachers for realistic and stressful working conditions. They offer practical expertise, awareness of school and personal functioning, and personal and professional development. Lack of adequate training will leave teachers to confront these issues of stress.

5.2   Conclusions

The findings in earlier chapters indicate that concerns over teacher-related stress have been growing in the last two decades, elevating the subject from the realms of "pop psychology to accredited research." Over 80 percent of the respondents had cause for stress and different reactions to stress in schools in Jamaica. This shows a considerable stress level of Jamaican teachers.

The investigation of causes of stress identified five major causes: lack of facilities, attitudes of students, salary received, lack of resources, and attitude to teachers. These results, in some way, reinforce the work of Kyriacou and Sutcliffe (1978a) as pupils' behavior and a major stress-producing problem. The writer suggests that this could be influenced by the total organization of the school. It is recommended that people concerned should start to revise the total operation of the school to suit the academic and social needs of the students.

Lack of facilities is another main concern, which Kyriacou and Sutcliffe (1978a) have identified as poor working conditions. This is a major cause of stress of Jamaican teachers. It is recommended that school organizations should examine and give careful attention to this issue so as to reduce its contribution to the existence of stress factors.

Other very important areas such as salary received, lack of resources, and attitudes to teachers, need close examination and attention so as to reduce the stress that teachers are experiencing.

The study also indicates five main areas of stress reaction: frustration, moodiness, feeling of exhaustion, tension, headache, and wanting to leave teaching. These findings are very similar to those of Dunham (1983). Frustration, which is the major reaction to stress of teachers in Jamaica, was also identified by Dunham (1983) as a major stress reaction. The writer suggests that these reactions to stress are influenced by the curriculum and the whole organization of the schools in Jamaica, and a definite and positive attitude should be taken to prevent these stress reactions.

There have been other reactions mentioned in the previous chapters which also give rise to concern. It is the writer's hope that every single aspect of stress reaction will be given keen consideration and attention.

Statistics show that although stress is evident throughout the occupational spectrum, particular facets of the work experience have been recognized as likely to increase the incidence of stress (MacKay and Cox, 1979). Conflict, which is inherent in the work task or within the work force, physical risk or perceived threat, which may be integral to the nature of the work or an inevitable consequence of it (such as risk of violence from parents), and frustrating repetitive or monotonous work have all been cited as stress inducers. My main conclusion is that excessive amounts of stress do undermine the quality of teachers' life. Indeed, it has shifted the focus on teachers' status from being a source of challenge and happiness to a "trap" for illness and premature death. Stress can and does precipitate serious dysfunctional effects. Stress disease and, particularly, coronary heart disease (CHD) are increasing in the Jamaican society and also here in the UK. Many of the causes are avoidable, but some are so much a part of modern organizational living that it is impossible for teachers to escape them. But unless we dig into the cause-effect relationship of the high-stress lifestyle of teachers, as I have tried to do, we will be constantly sheltered from the seriousness of the nature of the defects. Such evaluation can also help in explaining why the performance of loyal, hardworking, and valuable teachers may sometimes deteriorate rapidly. Nonetheless, it is also a conclusion that a certain amount of stress is useful in stimulating an individual to perform well at his job. However, we should avoid excessive amounts of it.

The important realization about stress is that the frequency, duration, and intensity of stressful experiences a person goes through are critical. In my view, recognition of the existence of teachers' stress has long been avoided at great cost to the school, teachers, their families, and friends. It seems that relying on the myth that mature and experienced people are able to cope in high-stress situations is shortsighted, unethical, and in the long-term uneconomical.

Stress affects workers at all levels of the school hierarchy; however, this work indicates that personal problem-solving and coping can be learned and developed and can be, indeed needs to be, supplemented by ongoing supports and organizational structures and policies.

It is clear to me that positive improvements are possible in the government's approach to teachers. Staff with high levels of training and skills required by schools needs active involvement with policy makers and decision making. These changes are necessary in order to promote a healthy teaching life.

Close links with heads to plan and develop school activities will ensure theory and practice are realistically integrated, promoting positive commitment to practice teaching; they may also foster a joint commitment to reducing teacher stress. I suggest it is not enough to increase the length of training; facilities must be committed to that training and value their roles. Real life and simulated experiences in applying expertise in the schools and interpersonal context are an essential part of teacher training.

As my results only made use of basic statistical techniques and involve a small sample which was spread out in five schools, caution must be exercised when drawing conclusions. Therefore, these results should be tested by more thorough investigations with far larger samples of teachers in each, or indeed, other types of schools, to give more weight to any final conclusion drawn. Only then could any realistic recommendations be made as to whether stress is more evident in Jamaica than the UK in order to both understand and reduce the amount of stress experienced before any real harm is done.

To make any future study more useful, and improve stress questionnaires with a wider range of responses, and written literature done by researchers, especially in Jamaica would give a far better indication of the amount, and type, of stress experienced, which could only improve the accuracy of my results.

Finally, it is hoped that the present study will stimulate further investigations into the little explored area to increase our understanding and knowledge of this extremely complex field.

Bibliography

Appley, M. H. and Trumbull, R. (1967). in Appleby M. H. and Trumbull, R. (Eds.) *On the Concept of Psychological Stress*. Psychological Stress, New York.

Argyle, M. (1974). *The Social Psychology of Work*. Penguin Books, UK, 1972.

Bandura, A. (1977). *A Social Learning Theory*. Prentice Hall, Upper Saddle River, NJ.

Blauner, R. (1964). *Alienation and Freedom*. University of Chicago Press, Chicago.

Bookbinder (1983). 'A new deal or dashed hopes'. *Special Education: Forward Trends*, Vol. 10, No. 1, pp. 6-7.

Braidwood, P. G. and Law, J. (1988). 'Stress'. *Observer Colour Supplement*, April 3, pp. 32-45.

Brennan, W. F. (1982). *Changing Special Education*. Open University Press, Milton Keyes.

Brown, A. (1986). 'The press and social work with reference to the Jasmine Beckford Case'. MA Soc Wk, UK.

Brown, P. (1986). 'Gender difference and mental health'. Unpublished paper, BA Hons, Middlesex Polytechnic.

Caplan, G. (1974). *Support Systems and Community*. Mental Health Behavioural Publications.

Cherniss, C. (1980). *Staff Burnout: Job Stress in the Human Service*. Sage Publication, Thousand Oaks, CA.

Clwyd County Council. (1976). *Absenteeism and Disruptive Behavior*. Clwyd County Council, England.

Cooper, C. C. and Marshall, J. (1976). 'Occupational sources of stress: a review of the literature relating to coronary heart disease and mental health'. *Journal Occupational Psychology*, Vol. 49, pp. 11-28.

Cox, T. (1975). 'The nature and management of stress'. *New Behavior*, 25 September, pp. 493-495.

Cox, T. G. and MacKay, C. J. (1976). *A Psychological Model of Occupational Stress: A Paper Presented to Medical Research Council Meeting*. Mental Health in Industry, London.

Cranwell-Ward, J. (1983). *Managing Stress*. Pan Books, German.

Dunham, J. (1981). 'Disruptive pupils and teacher stress'. *Educational Research*, Vol. 23, No. 3, pp. 205-13.

Dunham, J. (1983). 'Coping with stress in schools'. *Special Education: Forward Trends*, Vol. 10, No. 2.

Dunham, J. (1984). *Stress in Teaching*. Croom Helm, London.

Evans. K. M. (1962). *Sociometry and Education*. Routledge & Kegan Paul, London.

Farber, B. (1983). *Stress and Burnout in the Human Service Professions*. Pergamon Press, Oxford, UK.

Feitler, F. C. and Tokar, E. (1982). 'Getting a handle on teacher stress: How bad is the problem?' *Educational Leadership*, pp. 456-458.

Finman, M. J. (1982). 'What is teacher stress?' *Clearing House*, Vol. 56, No. 3, pp. 101-105.

Fineman, S. (1985) *Social Work Stress and Intervention*, Gower, London.

Fletcher, B. and Payne, R. (1982). 'Levels of reported stressors and strains amongst school teachers: Some UK data'. *Educational Review*, Vol. 34, No. 3.

Frude, N. G. and Gault, H. (Eds.) (1984). *Disruptive Behavior in Schools*. John Wiley & Sons, New York.

Gladthorpe, J. et al. (1986). *The Affluent Worker*. Cambridge University Press, Cambridge.

Gordon, B. (1981). *I Am Dancing As Fast As I Can*. Corgi, UK.

Growler, D. and Legge (Eds.) (1975). *Managerial Stress*. Gower Press, London.

Guest, D., Williams, R., and Dewe, P. (1978). *Job Design and the Psychology of Boredom*. WRU Occasional Paper No. 13.

Haddon, C. (1984). *Women and Tranquillizers*. Sheldon Press, London.

Handy, C. (1976). *Understanding Organizations*. Penguin Books, UK.

Hargreaves, D. H., Hester, S. K., and Mellor, F. J. (1975). *Deviance in Classroom*. Routledge and Kegan Paul Ltd., London.

Hawkins, K. (1979). *Textbook of Psychology*. Eastbourne-Saunders, UK.

Hendrickson, B. (1979). 'Teacher burnout: how to recognize it, what to do about it'. *Learning*, Vol. 7, No. 5, pp. 36-39.

Jones-Davies and Cave, R. G. (Eds.) (1976). 'The disruptive pupil in the secondary level'. *Warlock Educational.*

Instructor Survey (1972), *Instructor*, Vol. 86, No. 6, p. 12.

Kyriacou, C. (1980). 'Coping actions and occupational stress among school teachers'. *Research in Education*, No. 24, pp. 57-61.

Kyriacou, C. (1981). 'Social support and occupational stress among school teachers'. *Educational Studies*, Vol. 7, No. 1, pp. 55-60.

Kyriacou, C. (1987). 'Teacher stress and burnout: an international review'. *Educational Research*, Vol. 29, No. 2, pp. 146-52.

Kyriacou, C. G. and Sutcliffe, J. (1975). 'Teacher stress. Prevalence, sources and symptoms'. *British Journal of Education*, Vol. 46, pp. 159-67.

Kyriacou, C. G. and Sutcliffe, J. (1977). 'Teacher stress: a review'. *Educational Review*, Vol. 29, pp. 299-306.

Kyriacou, C. and Sutcliffe, J. (1978a). 'A model of teacher stress'. *Educational Studies*, Vol. 4, pp. 1-6.

Kyriacou, C. and Sutcliffe, J. (1978b). 'Teacher stress prevalence, source and symptoms'. *BJET*, Vol. 48, pp. 159-167.

Kyriacou, C. and Sutcliffe, J. (1979). 'A note on teacher stress locus of control'. *Journal of Occupational Psychology*, Vol. 52, pp. 227-8.

La Haye, T. (1983). *How to Manage Pressure before Pressure Manages You.* Marshalls Paperbacks, Barrington, IL.

Lazarus, R. S. (1966). *Psychological Stress and the Coping Process.* McGraw-Hill, New York.

Lazarus, R. S. (1976). *Pattern of Adjustment.* McGraw-Hill, New York.

Lloyd Smith, M. (1984). *Disruptive Schooling (The Growth of the Special Unit)*. Murray, London.

MacKay, C. G. and Cox, T. (Eds.) (1979). *Response to Stress. Occupational Aspects*. IPC Press, London.

Maclure, S. (1988). *Education Reformed. Times Educational Supplement*. Hodder & Stoughton, London.

Marland, M. (1975). *The Craft of the Classroom*. Heinemann, London.

Maslach, C. and Jackson, S. E. (1981). 'The measurement of experienced burnout'. *Journal of Occupational Behavior*, Vol. 2, pp. 99-113.

McGarth, J. E. (1970). *Social Psychological Factor in Stress*. Holt, Rinehart and Winston, California.

Needle, R. H. et al. (1980). 'Teacher stress, sources and consequences'. *Journal of Scottish Health*, pp. 96-99.

Pepitone, A. (1967). 'Self social environment and stress', in Appley, M. H. and Trumbull, R. (Eds.) *Psychological Stress*. Appleton Century Crafts, New York.

Pratt, J. (1978). 'Perceived stress among teachers: the effect of age and background of children taught'. *Educational Review*, Vol. 30, pp. 3-14.

Sayles, L. and Strauss, G. (1966). *Human Behavior in Organization*. Prentice Hall, Upper Saddle River, NJ.

Schwab, R. L. and Iwanicki, E. F. (1980). 'Who are burned out teachers?' *Educational Research Quarterly* 1982, Vol. 7, No. 2, pp 5-15.

Schwab, R. L. (1983). 'Teacher burnout moving beyond "psychobabble".' *Theory into Practice*, Vol. 22, No. 1, pp. 21-26.

Seyle, H. (1956). *Stress of Life*. McGraw-Hill, New York.

Seyle, H. (1974). *Stress without Distress*. New American Library, New York.

Seyle, H. (1975). 'Confusion and controversy in stress'. *Field Journal Human Stress*, Vol. 1, p. 37.

Simpson, B. (1987). 'Pummeling dummies'. *One Solution for Stress*. Executive Post No. 370, p. 3.

Smith, G. (1970). *Social Work and the Sociology of Organizations*. Routledge and Kegan Paul, London.

Spaniol, R. G. and Caputo, T. (1978). 'From who are burned out teachers?' *Educational Research Quarterly* 1982, Vol. 7, No. 2, pp 5-16.

Tapp, S. (1986). 'What are the elements of stress in families looking after mentally handicapped young adults and might it be eased?', MA Soc Wk, UK.

Warnock Report (1978). *Special Educational Needs: Report of the Committee of Enquiry into the Education of Handicapped Children and Young People*. HMSO, London.

Appendix I

Questionnaire

This questionnaire is required for research that is being carried out into stress experienced by teachers. The information given will be treated with strictest confidence. There is no right or wrong answer to the questions. All that is required of you is that you answer the questions as truthfully as possible.

Please tick the appropriate answers unless otherwise specified.

1. Gender   male [ ] Female [ ]
2. Teaching Experience in years   0-5 [ ] 6-10 [ ]
                                              11-15 [ ] 16-20 [ ]
                                              21 and over [ ]
3. Please state position held in school   _____
4. Number of years in present position   0-5 [ ] 6-10 [ ]
                                              11-15 [ ] 16-20 [ ]
                                              21 and over [ ]
5. Level of Qualification   Teachers Training
                                              Diploma
                                              P G C E
                                              Other

6. If the answer to question 5 was other, please specify _____
7. My training was in

    Primary Education [ ]
    Secondary Education [ ]
    Special Education [ ]
    Nursery Education [ ]

8. Please specify what sort of in-service courses or upgrading courses teachers in your school are currently undergoing

    _____
    _____
    _____
    _____

9. Do you consider the initial training you received in terms of dealing with students as

    Very adequate [ ]
    Reasonably adequate [ ]
    Not sure [ ]
    Not very adequate [ ]

10. What would make you feel better able to cope with incidents involving conflicts either with students or staff?

    Please specify.
    Personal skills _____
    _____
    School policies _____
    _____
    None _____

Please tick any of the following which causes stress.

1. Lack of facilities   [ ]
2. School buildings   [ ]
3. Attitude of teachers   [ ]
4. Attitude of students   [ ]
5. Salary received   [ ]
6. Position held   [ ]
7. Bureaucracy   [ ]
8. Absenteeism of colleagues   [ ]

9. Advisors   [ ]
10. Parents   [ ]
11. Lack of resources   [ ]
12. School Organization   [ ]
13. Duties   [ ]
14. Excessive number of meetings   [ ]
15. Conflicts between home and work demands   [ ]
16. Others—(Please specify)   _____

                                     _____

                                     _____

                                     _____

                                     _____

These have been found to be common reactions to stress experienced by teachers.

Please put a tick next to any of the following reactions to work stress that you have experienced over the past year.

1. Depression   [ ]
2. Moodiness   [ ]
3. Inability   [ ]
4. Poor concentration   [ ]
5. Absenteeism   [ ]
6. Tension Headaches   [ ]
7. Frustration   [ ]
8. Feeling of exhaustion   [ ]
9. Withdrawal from staff contact   [ ]
10. Anxiety   [ ]
11. Anger   [ ]

12. Skin rash   [ ]

13. Disturbed sleep   [ ]

14. Feeling of isolation in schools   [ ]

15. Feeling of fear   [ ]

16. Feeling of guilt   [ ]

17. Wanting to leave teaching   [ ]

18. Unwilling to support colleagues   [ ]

19. Uncomfortable confrontation with parents   [ ]

20. Marked reduction of contacts with pupils outside school   [ ]

21. Displaced aggression, displacement onto children, colleagues, or pupils outside school   [ ]

22. Feeling of being unable to cope   [ ]

23. Apathy   [ ]

24. Irritability   [ ]

25. Feeling of inferiority   [ ]

26. Increased drinking   [ ]

27. Increased smoking   [ ]

28. Increased eating   [ ]

Thank You for your cooperation.